Evolve!

With the

WISDOM WHISPERER

More Insider Career Secrets From Your Virtual Mentor

Second in a Series

by Kathleen E.R. Murphy

Evolve!

With the

WISDOM WHISPERER

ISBN: 9781710338003

Wordsmith: Kathleen Veth

Editing, Design, and Composition: Cheryl L. Cromer
Square Moon Publishing Solutions LLC
Square-Moon.com

| Praise for *Wisdom Whisperer* |

Kathleen Murphy possesses many unique insights into how real people interact every day. In this book, she demonstrates the complex power and potential available in your workplace, and some of the layers getting in the way. Her deep mastery of relationship and leadership principles is embedded in highly perceptive observations. Each page delivers practical wisdom for building productive, effective teams and for reducing the inevitable friction that comes from bringing different personalities and talents together.

— Luke Bayly, Gallup Certified Strengths Coach, North of Sydney, Australia

I loved chapter one and can't wait to read the rest. I would definitely recommend Evolve! With the Wisdom Whisperer to anyone one who aspires to or is currently in a leadership role. It will give you the confidence to handle mentoring and leadership situations.

— Chris Bower, Banking CEO, Oklahoma

In Evolve!, Kathleen E. R. Murphy, author of Wisdom Whisperer and Founder/CEO of Market Me Too, demystifies the school of thought that leaders are born with emotional intelligence. Not your typical 'how to become a leader' book, it's chock-full of tips, insights, and proven advice based on real-world examples taken from leading global organizations. Narrated in an impactful storytelling fashion, present and future leaders alike will acquire practical and immediately actionable steps to a successful career.

— Ron Draper, CEO, Fortune 100 Bank, Boston

Kathy Murphy shares her well-earned wisdom in business and life through engaging stories with lessons for all of us. The depth of subject matter and the volume of highly relevant words with practical tips makes this a book that everyone should keep on their bedside table.

— Kat Frati, Cape Elizabeth, Maine

In person Kathy imparts wisdom and inspires greatness in those around her. This book is an honest reflection and extension of her. She shares thought-provoking insights to help people reflect on their current roles in business and life, and inspires confidence and development to support you in achieving your goals.

— Rachel E.R. Neighbour, London

Kathleen Murphy is the professional colleague and navigator you wish you had on your team to guide you. Now you do. In her second book, Evolve! With the Wisdom Whisperer, she candidly shares her extensive years of insightful business experience, thoughtfully communicated via a mixture of realistic professional and personal advice. Murphy's book is helpful, easy to read and digest. It is perfect for anyone looking to further cultivate both their professional and personal lives.

— Ellen O'Brien, Recording Artist/Voice Coach, and CEO, Ellen O'Brien Music, New York

|| More Praise for *Wisdom Whisperer* ||

This is a great read that reveals lessons learned in the professional world. Murphy covers topics ranging from leadership, vulnerability, storytelling, and motivation. Through raw stories, Murphy shares her experiences and challenges you to reflect upon your own. This book is easy-to-read, thought-provoking, and inspirational.

— Kayla Regan, Boston

These pages are a powerful read as the words will conjure up things within yourself you may realize need to be addressed in order to become the complete person you are capable of being. It's not about highlighting faults; it's about discovering what may be holding you back and giving you the tools to be better. Kathleen Murphy is an all-around woman who is very accomplished, astute, clever, intuitive, and inquisitive. These qualities make her not only a "people person," but one who can navigate, negotiate, motivate and ..."get it done!" She shares these skills in her book with what I feel is now the most important aspect of success...recognizing and embracing one's vulnerability toward becoming a strong leader, and all the supporting cast members of a business team. If you want to get a hold of your future, you first must harness your dreams. In Evolve! With the Wisdom Whisperer, you will be well on your way to doing so.

— Lark Logan, Boston

Author Kathleen Murphy charts a pathway to progressive leadership development with a passionate explication of how, what, and why anyone who aspires to become a leader should endeavor to be a "great leader." Leadership is not about self, it is about service and commitment to others; therefore, the leader must understand people and to do so, he or she must understand him or herself well to model humanity and humility. As an author, Kathleeen has and continues to share her insights, experience, and support on leadership development via various written platforms. That accessibility allows for others to engage her directly.

— Dwight B. Sanchez, Vice President, Enrollment Management
Virginia Union University, Richmond

This book is designed for a wide audience ranging from an early career person learning about leadership characteristics to the most experienced at leading. Kathleen Murphy puts a challenging and engaging blueprint into print for leaders at any stage.

— Jason Solomon, Strategy Executive, Boston

‖ Acknowledgements ‖

The fact I am publishing my second book is hard for me to believe. I could not have accomplished this project without the continuous support and encouragement from my husband Stephen Shinnick, and our three children, Maxwell Shinnick, Bronwyn Shinnick, and Cole Shinnick. Of course, I also have to mention Ollie, our 8-year-old Goldendoodle, who is usually by my side when I am writing.

There are two incredible women I also need to recognize who played roles in bringing this second book to life. The first is Kathleen Veth, who has worked on both of my books. Although Kathleen likes to refer to herself as a proofreader, I tell her that no matter what she wishes to be called, I think of her as a make-up artist for my words. The second incredible woman who also made my books come to life is Cheryl Cromer. Cheryl acts as publisher, editor, and design guru. Most importantly, she keeps me sane during the overwhelming process people unfamiliar with publishing a book are not aware of.

I would also like to thank my parents, Daniel I. Murphy, Jr., and Emily R. Murphy, for playing their obvious roles, and for believing in me and encouraging me to keep writing.

And my thanks to those who either inspired me, or contributed ideas for some of my stories (knowingly or unknowingly): Marty Beecy (hairstylist), Andrew Brearton, Maureen Electa-Monte, Nancy Federici, Myra Hart, Mark Hedtler, Mike Howell, Stephanie Jimenez (Public Relations), Julius Johnson, Ellie Kai (Front Cover Dress), Doug Kennedy, Michelle Kessler-Sanders, Holden Laquerre, **Dave Marchand (personal trainer)**, Catherine R. Murphy, Christopher J. Murphy, Ellen O'Brien, Lori Reyna, Jacqueline Shaw, Sophie Shaw (makeup artist), Joseph T. Shinnick, Jill Schmidt (Public Relations), Anna Maria Soriano, Thomas G. Stemberg, Patrick Sweeney, and Kathrine Thomas (photographer).

— *Kathleen E.R. Murphy*

| About the Author |

Author and Market Me Too Founder and CEO Kathleen E.R. Murphy is known for radiating enthusiasm, positive energy, and a highly creative problem-solving acumen. Many have referred to her as a business and sports team "muse."

Kathleen's executive management career has spanned more than 25 years, focusing on marketing technology at companies such as APC, Black Duck, Constant Contact, Hitachi, and EMC/Dell, as well as at start-up companies in a variety of industries. Kathleen is a globally recognized motivational speaker and Gallup Strengths Performance Coach, and regularly blogs and leads workshops on leadership, business, and career management. Additionally, Kathleen is an inspirational speaker and social commentator and influencer. She credits her family lineage of inventors and entrepreneurs for shaping her career path.

Since 2016, Kathleen has been a highly sought-after mentor in the United States Women Unlimited Executive Mentor Program. She has mentored five Babson College MBA students, and hundreds of individuals during her career. She works with individuals ages 14-100+ (her Nana lived to 102) at all business levels, from those just starting out in their careers to c-suite executives and teams. In addition, she uses her strengths-based coaching expertise to help sports teams and athletes achieve their performance goals.

In 2019, Kathleen was appointed an Advisory Board Member to the Undergraduate and Graduate Business Schools at her alma mater, the University of Maine, where she earned her undergraduate degree in Journalism with a minor in Psychology. In April 2019, she was named Chairwoman of the Board of Directors for the Spring 2020 Merrimack Valley Women's Conference.

Kathleen has been published in *Advancing Women, AskTheExpert, Boston Voyager, Fast Company, The Huffington Post, i4Business, Money, Readers Digest, Recruiter, The Economist, Thrive Global,* and *U.S. News and World Report.* Since 2018, she has been a featured guest on a number of popular business television and radio shows. Her TV show and podcast, "Murf & E Unfiltered – Zero B.S. Biz Talk," launched in July 2019.

Evolve! With the Wisdom Whisperer is the second in a series. Kathleen's first book, *Wisdom Whisperer,* published in April 2018 by Amazon, shares secrets and insights to success in business and life from lessons learned in her 20s, 30s, and 40s as an upcoming executive and full-time working mother. Kathleen is currently working on her third and fourth books, which will be published in the fall of 2020 and 2021. To learn more about Market Me Too and how Kathleen can help your company, visit MarketMeToo.net or email her at KathyMurphy@me.com.

Evolve!
With the WISDOM WHISPERER

|| Table of Contents ||

Chapter 3 | Work Tips

Chapter 4 | Life Tips

|| Introduction ||

The fact that I'm publishing my second book is, in my mind, short of another small miracle. In the introduction of my first book, *Wisdom Whisperer*, I talked about how I had to overcome Imposter Syndrome, and leverage my top StrengthsFinder 2.0 strength of Positivity to become an entrepreneur and author. Mission accomplished!

One of the driving forces behind why I continue to craft and produce content is because I am so passionate about helping and leading others in the workforce. I did not have an official mentor when I was climbing up the proverbial business ladder. I sure wish I did. In my first book, the story of "Who's Your Mentor" reinforces the importance of having others support and mentor you.

After I published my first book, I never imagined it would open up so many new doors of opportunity for me. One of them was being asked to join the University of Maine Business School Advisory Board (Undergraduate and Graduate). This was followed by appearing on a series of radio and local area television shows to talk about my book, and professionally speaking at workshops and conferences around the country.

In May 2019, I was asked to become the Chairwoman of a local area women's conference (Merrimack Valley Women's Conference). In July, I launched my first TV Show and podcast, "Murf & E Unfiltered – Zero B.S. Biz Talk." These are only a few of the opportunities that my book *Wisdom Whisperer* offered me. My point is that these activities will fuel and shape the contents of my other books, and allow me to continue to serve as a "virtual mentor" for people all around the globe.

Speaking of our world, nothing makes my day brighter than when I hear from people who are positively impacted by my writing. Although my book is currently available only in English, I regularly hear from readers outside of the United States — Africa (Kenya, Liberia, Mauritius, Morocco, Namibia, Nigeria, South Africa, Sudan, Tanzania, Tunisia, Uganda), Australia, Bahamas, Bermuda, Brazil, Canada, China, Europe (Denmark, Faroe Islands, Finland, France, Germany, Guernsey, Greece, Ireland, Italy, Latvia, Poland, Netherlands, Spain, Sweden, Switzerland, United Kingdom), Kitts & Nevis, India (Bangladesh, Bhutan), Indonesia, Japan, Malaysia, Mexico, the Middle East (Bahrain, Egypt, Iraq, Israel, Lebanon, Pakistan, Saudi Arabia, United Arab Emirates), New Zealand, Peru, Philippines, Romania, Russia (Kyrgyzstan), Singapore, Slovenia, South Korea, Sri Lanka, Taiwan, Trinidad & Tobago, and Vietnam. Someday it would be amazing to meet all of my readers both abroad and in the U.S.

Based on assembling this list, perhaps a cross country or global book and speaking tour is in my future? Or, perhaps a nationally or internationally syndicated show? Don't worry, I'm planning on it, but I might need some help from my professional "tribe" who serve as my mentors. Yes, I have a number of mentors, too.

The other driving force behind my writing is to help inspire, engage, and motivate people. If you are not familiar with my writing style, you will learn that I challenge and take people out of their comfort zones. I also ask them to consider thinking or acting differently.

Welcome to my second book, *Evolve! With the Wisdom Whisperer.* When I first started blogging, I never imagined I would turn my blogs into a book — not to mention a second one! And in January 2020, I will start writing book number five. Yes, that's right, my fifth book. So, if you like this one, and I hope you do, in 2021 and the years following it you will have more of them to read.

For those of you who are challenged with finding time to improve your personal or professional life, and are looking for leadership and your own virtual mentor, you found one — me! I'm glad you found me.

I am the Wisdom Whisperer, and I'll be on this journey with you. Now let's get started!

Chapter 1 | Work

|| Leadership and Vulnerability ||

Being vulnerable in business might sound counterintuitive, especially since many people think about business as analogous to an Olympic sport where winning is the ultimate goal. But allowing employees to see your softer side is one of the things that ultimately will make you a better leader, and your company more competitive.

It's given that business leaders need to be hard-nosed and competitive. But leaders should also exhibit a sense of compassion for their employees. Leaders who show their human side are more approachable.

Some of the most effective leaders I have worked for, and with, share a few characteristics, but all of them understand the importance of commanding respect while simultaneously being open to showing a softer side when interacting with their teams. Indeed, this is one of the most endearing and important traits that makes people want to follow a leader.

If you are a leader, work for one, or want to be one, think about whether you or your leader possesses this quality. Perhaps they do, but you only get a glimpse of it, and not consistently. Now imagine what it would be like to work — or be — this kind of leader.

Some people take on a different persona at work. Are you a big bad wolf at the office and a cuddly teddy bear at home? As Dr. Phil would ask, "How's that workin' for ya?"

Or do you develop leadership qualities based on being collaborative and approachable, allowing your natural ability of high emotional intelligence to flourish.

Unfortunately, emotional intelligence is not something that can be taught; it can, however, be mimicked. If you feel you are lacking, pay attention to those who do. For example, watch as successful leaders properly greet a guest and make them feel comfortable, or ask someone who seems sad or upset if they need to take a moment, or want to talk.

Leaders who are open to the human experience are in no way weak. Sometimes we conveniently forget that our leaders are human, too, and typically under constant pressure. Having to mask their emotions is difficult, but doing so is not a sign of weakness. When business leaders reveal that they are experiencing emotions, it sends signals to the people who work for them that they are simply human. This makes them more approachable.

Often, however, when a leader exhibits emotion, many people are either simply oblivious, or if they do notice, don't comment. Most are probably reluctant to approach the boss. It's okay to ask how they are doing, and do so sincerely. You might be surprised by the reaction you get. Be prepared to respond in a kind and empathetic manner. This sentiment will be appreciated more than you can imagine. What's more, the leader will perceive you in an entirely different light the next time you interact. Why? Because you allowed them to be themselves for that moment — rarely something many leaders feel like they can or should be.

Climbing up the proverbial corporate ladder can take years, but some people reach the top faster than others. Although many factors come into play, one is that they are likeable. And part of being likeable is being human. Typically these people are also bright, and have a personality that makes others believe in and want to follow them.

Of course, this is an over simplification of the other criteria one needs to climb the rungs. Typically, it is much harder for those who reached the top because of an inside connection to earn the respect of their team. Authentic leaders who have earned the right to be placed into leadership roles are the ones whom we admire, potentially aspire to be like, and ultimately respect and want to follow.

|| Storytelling ||

Storytelling, and the ability to do it well, is part art and part science. The artistry is in the form of the words chosen to illustrate a story, while the science is in the formula and the method you use to convey your message. Doing it well can open many doors both personally as well as professionally. How well can you tell your story?

When I was growing up, one of the treats I enjoyed most was listening to stories told to me by my grandparents. All of them were raised during the depression, before the technologies we commonly accept were available — cell phones, Internet, even television (and definitely robots). The stories they told were often about their childhood or as young adults with new careers. I was always fascinated by their tales, which they infused with colorful examples, and often, their feelings. Looking back, the best part was when they expressed the impact a particular experience had on them. Listening to their stories was like watching a 3-D movie, but better!

My paternal grandfather was a Massachusetts State Police Officer. My maternal grandfather was employed by Polaroid. Both worked at these jobs their entire careers, and each of them had unique stories that came to life through the rise and fall of their voices. Their descriptions of the people involved and how they interacted with them left me on the edge of my seat. There was no possibility of being distracted when they were telling you their stories. I never wanted them to end!

My two grandfathers were exceptional storyteller role models. The art and science of telling an exceptional story is something which can take years to master. I am still working to refine this skill myself. Part of learning how to become a great storyteller is to keep in mind the basic elements — incorporating a beginning, middle, and end, and including the who, what, where, when, why, and how of the tale. If you disregard any of these elements, the story will not seem complete, and the listener could be confused with what you are trying to express.

Exceptional story tellers also build their story from a whisper to a roar. They try to include the audience in the story whenever possible, bringing them along for the journey. Storytelling is one of the foundational pillars of communication. The skills required to do so can be obtained through drafts, edits, and practice.

Some of my favorite storytellers are those who share stories about history. Recently I was listening to an exceptional storyteller as he took the audience through the various uses of a coconut. What I learned was that essentially every part of a coconut is utilized in some way, which he demonstrated during the course of his 10-minute lecture. He assured listeners that we could survive on an island for quite a period of time if we had access to coconuts, as they would provide both food and liquid. We learned that we could use coconuts fronds to make hats, baskets, roofs, mats, toys, even clothing. He then carved the coconut and offered samples of coconut juice to some lucky audience members. Before I sampled the juice, I did not think I liked it; however, knowing more about this item made me consider it in a different way, and this is one of the key results to a great storyteller's abilities.

Everyone has the ability to be a strong storyteller, but it takes practice, preparation, and concentration to ensure you cover the foundational elements. Once you're ready for an audience, pay attention to the cadence of your voice, as many people speak too quickly or softly when they present to an audience. The best way to judge your own performance is to record yourself (on video, if possible). If you're like most people, you will soon notice where you can improve your presentation. Take notes so you can improve upon your technique and ability.

Using your storytelling abilities in both life and business will serve you well. Next time someone in upper management tells a story, see if they have perfected the art and science of this skill.

| Building A Girls Club |

The "Good Ol' Boys Club" has been in existence for years, but isn't it curious such a club doesn't exist for women? Men have arguably been much better at networking and supporting each other in business than women. And although they're slowly doing a better job, women need to step up our game and do a better job of supporting one another.

I'm not sure if there is an unwritten rule or if it is in their DNA to naturally help one another, but men seem to do so remarkably better than women in supporting one another in business. Why is this happening, and what can women do to become better at helping one another?

In the last dozen years, I have worked to coach women to become better at recognizing that they need to support one another, and how to do so. Helping other women in business does not seem to come naturally to many women, despite the fact most females are, by nature, nurturing and empathetic. However, when they are put into competitive or business scenarios, they tend not to utilize these skills as much as they might ordinarily do in non-business situations.

I am all for competition, but one of the things that has frustrated me the most is seeing women, whether they realize it or not, sabotaging the success of other women instead of working with them to help them achieve more success. Not all women do this, but I have seen far too many who are blatantly guilty, and it needs to be course corrected. If you are a woman, are you guilty of this; or if you are a man, have you witnessed this kind of behavior? In either instance, to truly be equal with our male counterparts, women need to take a stance on embracing the concept of helping other women to be successful. The first step is to recognize their failure.

Historians have documented the trials and tribulations women have had to endure to compete on equal terms. And we still have more work to do in order to fully share in the advantages our male colleagues have, and continue, to enjoy. Women can reach equality with male peers, but first need to stop hurting and instead start helping our female peers. Here are ways to be more collaborative with your female business peers.

1| Any time we set out to fix or change something, we need to first admit there is a challenge facing us. Are we treating our female colleagues differently than we do our male colleagues? Organize a group of women to get together to discuss if they recognize their need to play a critical role in working towards helping one another. Consider expanding your female professional network with women from your industry or others to leverage ideas or discuss challenges they see that are not supportive of women's professional success.

2| Once we admit we have a challenge, we must then commit to a resolution. Are we fully supporting our female colleagues in a positive manner? Identify two to three women in your immediate business that you can work with to help make them more successful. Create a list of what you can do personally to help your women business peers, or women who are in your network that can benefit from your assistance. Set goals for the women you are working with to help bolster their success, and meet monthly to benchmark progress.

3| Reach out to more experienced businesswomen and ask for help in becoming stronger and more successful in your career.

4| The best way to get to know people better is to spend quality time with them. Commit to informal meetings with women at your company outside of work to get to know one another.

5| Challenge yourself to being part of solving the challenge of women not being as good as our male peers at helping and supporting one another's success.

Helping others is one of the most noble things you can do. As women, we need to recognize our lack of support for our female peers. Let's change this for our daughters, nieces, and other young females in the workplace and create our own "Girls Club."

|| Satisfaction ||

When I hear The Rolling Stones sing 'Satisfaction,' it conjures up a number of different meanings. How about you? Is being satisfied a goal, or are there varying degrees of being satisfied in a professional career?

Should satisfaction be something to aim for when discussing your career? Or, does it mean that when you are satisfied with your current career, the level you have attained, or the industry you are in, you can hit the snooze button and show up in robot mode every day?

To me, being satisfied seems like a mediocre level of attainment when it is associated with an expression of how you feel. Wouldn't you rather be more excited and motivated by your career rather than only okay with it?

Being satisfied might, in fact, be a reasonable achievement for many people when discussing their career, but I have to imagine there was a point in time when this may not have been acceptable.

If this were the case, what was it that made them wake up one day and say, "I am satisfied with my career and what I have accomplished, so I am not going to continue to go beyond where I am."

Is this a sad declaration of giving up, or are they only taking a break and satisfaction is an acceptable place at which to plateau?

I would like to think being satisfied is a temporary status, and one that allows the individual to recharge to catapult to the next level. Kind of like if you were climbing a mountain and stopped to rest and rejuvenate your body at various elevations along the way to the summit.

Speaking of summits, when I was at EMC, now Dell/EMC, I ran a sales promotion program called *Journey to the Top*. The mission was to entice our partners to sell more of our products and services and be rewarded with a wide variety of prizes from which to choose. What surprised me the most about this promotion was the type of prizes people chose, most of which were quite practical and which I thought no one would ever pick.

I was so wrong in my estimation about which rewards would be the most popular. Thankfully, I heeded the advice of the promotion company I was working with to include non-flashy options like pots and pans, diapers, microwaves, and winter jackets. People were satisfied with practical items they did not have to spend their own money on, and bypassed the flashy, more glamorous prizes they could have just as easily chosen.

The fact that the less sexy and more practical rewards were chosen over the much cooler and harder-to-attain prizes, even though they could have chosen them, was a great lesson. It demonstrated how you can be surprised by what people are satisfied with, and that it is not always as hard as you think it might be for folks to attain satisfaction.

When I asked our partners about why they opted to pick the practical versus the more interesting, they told me they wanted to have something to keep striving for, and that they would initially be more satisfied with the practical choices. They told me if they selected the more interesting prizes initially, that they were concerned about losing their motivation about the promotion. Interestingly, these partners were practiced in the art of long-term gratification. They knew that instant reward is not always the right approach, and does not guarantee any level of real satisfaction.

Circling back to whether it is acceptable to be simply satisfied with your current career status, the response should actually be . . . it depends.

It depends on whether you are the kind of person who is highly motivated and always striving for the next level, or the kind of person who has not thought much about whether you should be satisfied with your career level. If you are more in alignment with this type of thinking, then you will either at some point be satisfied, or realize you need to do something different.

Going through the motions of showing up at work and not obtaining any positive reinforcement from what you are doing, other than a steady paycheck and benefits, will at some point wake you up to the fact there is a whole world out there that may offer you greater career satisfaction.

Sometimes the grass is, in fact, greener on the other side; but not always. You will know when you get there, as you will often find yourself peering through the proverbial fence to the other side.

‖ Pride in Your Work ‖

Taking pride in your work, no matter what you do, is important. Your work is an extension and outward representation of who you are. If your work is not easily seen, understood, or appreciated, it is even more important for you to be able to verbally express pride in what you do. Have you shared your work pride with others?

Many people have had all types of jobs, including short-term jobs, part-time work, contract positions for earning extra cash, and eventually, a career of choice. Some of the most interesting work I have heard about is intangible, clarified only by the person who was able to articulate in detail, and with enormous pride, the steps they took and what they accomplished.

Regardless of the kind of job you have had, be proud of what you are doing! Tell others about your work. Many people do not talk much about their work. But when you talk about your job accomplishments, you begin to smile and shine, and become more interesting.

One of the things I vividly recall from childhood is how my father did not talk about his job. Like my grandfather, he was employed by Polaroid, but I really had no idea what he did there. When I asked Dad about it, he would respond with limited and vague information. He was also a master of changing the subject when I was putting him through my daily interrogation routine. I probably drove him crazy with the questions I would ask him to see if I could discover any details, but I was never able to extract enough information to understand. After a while of bombarding him with questions, I stopped asking, and concluded he must be a spy. It was easier to think he was a Double Agent and to appreciate the idea he worked in a government security role and that was why he could not tell me about his job.

I would imagine 99 percent of people are not spies, so you should be able to talk about your job with others. Fortunately, Dad is still alive, so I can continue to try and get some information from him about his job at Polaroid. Perhaps now, since enough time has passed, and much of the information has probably been declassified, he can talk about some of the work he did. Or at least I think about it that way. The point is to not give up on someone who either does not want to talk about their job, or is uncomfortable doing so.

Even though not all jobs sound glamourous, there are aspects to every occupation that make them interesting. The trick is to figure out what aspects of your job makes you interesting, and be able to explain them to anyone who asks, "What do you do?"

One of the things I find most interesting about meeting and talking to new people is to learn about all of the different jobs that exist. Think about someone you recently met, who has a very different job than yours. Did you find their work and how they described it interesting? Did you learn anything from what they shared? Did you know that such a job even existed?

On a recent trip to Fiji, I met a basil farmer, two gold market traders, and a masseuse/hairstylist. I also shared a conversation with a former advertising executive who worked at a prestigious agency in Paris, and another person who worked in a research role in Australia to determine how to improve the lives of their veterans. It was obvious as they told me about their jobs that each of these people took immense pride in the work they did.

At first, you may think there's little about your work that makes you proud; but there is always something positive in any situation. I challenge you to think about one or two things that make you proud of your work. Having even just a few things you can share with others about why you like your job will make a difference in how you approach the "daily grind."

Your sense of pride will also positively influence how others perceive you. You could be considered for a promotion or asked to take on a new role, or perhaps a challenge you had not considered.

| Setting Expectations |

One of the hard lessons I learned early in my career was to set proper expectations on any commitment you take on. In the sales world, this is referred to as an upfront contract. When both parties are in agreement with what will be accomplished, it makes the work slightly less stressful, and typically produces an outcome that ensures both parties will be satisfied with the results. Do you set upfront contracts to set proper expectations?

Any time you are about to embark upon a new task, pause for a moment. Ask yourself if both you and the parties involved with the assignment are truly on the same page, and that you agree to what the end results and deliverables should be. Doing this before you begin greatly improves the chance of success.

First, put expectations in writing to eliminate any ambiguity that can result from verbal agreements. This is one of the reasons all contracts are put into writing. As the written agreements are passed between the parties, there is the opportunity to go back and forth and edit the document so everyone is in agreement about an expected outcome. This will mitigate the risk of any unplanned and negative surprises.

When written agreements are being formalized, allow a few days to let the document "breathe" before making the final edits. Taking time to separate yourself from the document details for a day or two will allow you to gauge how complete the communication is, or what critical elements may have been overlooked.

One project I took on shortly after accepting a marketing role at a technology company included reviewing the contracts and projects associated with trade shows to which the previous job holder had committed. I determined there was one show for which the person had signed a contract nine months earlier. This meant I had just three months to work on a project that normally would take about six to eight months of preparation. Since I knew how much work was involved, and withdrawing from the contract was not financially feasible, I had to determine the best way to set the right expectations for my boss about how our company was going to successfully exhibit at this trade show.

The first thing I did was to create a schedule working backwards, with a realistic timeline about what I could accomplish in three months. Having years of experience allowed me to be able to design a realistic strategic execution plan, but I knew I was going to need more help to pull this off.

Part of putting the working execution schedule together included communicating that I would need additional budget to hire a part-time person to help me with the tactical work, as I focused on the strategic portion and branding aspects. By detailing what elements of the project would need to be accomplished, I was able to exhibit for my boss the work required for a successful outcome. My boss was satisfied with understanding what would be realistic to achieve in the timeframe, and we were able to negotiate from the plan.

My reverse schedule also included, in writing, which specific elements of this project were not feasible. We also shared this detailed plan with the executive management and sales teams, and obtained their support so everyone was in agreement with the final expectations.

Thanks to a solid and agreed-to upfront contract with my boss, the executive management, and sales team, by the time we were on the trade show exhibit floor, everyone was pleased. The best part is the fact I over delivered by 200% on the initial expectations I had set. What's more, I won a company award for flawless execution of a project most people thought was impossible to pull off.

The key element associated with the success of this project was keeping everyone on the big-picture team aligned from the beginning on what could be realistically achieved, and allowing everyone to do their part to help make the project successful. In essence, this was also an example of supreme collaboration, with the underpinning of setting proper expectations up front.

| Office Relationships |

As I write this, there have been more than a dozen public figures who have been labeled as having had inappropriate relationships with co-workers, employees, or subordinates. I sense these announcements are like the waves of what appears to be an oncoming tsunami of social change. Seems like a great time to consider office relationships.

I am writing on the topic of office relationships, platonic or romantic, based upon more than two decades witnessing these scenarios playing out in corporate America, as well as in offices in Europe and Asia.

Personally, I have never crossed the line when it comes to mixing work and relationships; however, I have seen numerous colleagues do this, and it has prompted me to create a pros and cons list for readers.

When I first started working, social media and online dating didn't exist. If you wanted to engage socially, or find someone to date, you had to meet them at social events, through friends, family, bars, religious gatherings, or at activities where attendees shared some common interest such as hiking or sporting events. In some ways, it was easier to meet people and engage, as you had a chance to interact in a multi-dimensional way. You were forced to apply all your human senses when face to face. You could also quickly determine if you were attracted to them in person, so this sped up the process of narrowing your choices.

Our online world has not caught up to being able to introduce all aspects of a multi-dimensional meeting. Until it is able to introduce the affects of pheromones into the meeting equation, people will have to continue to vet and meet one another in person. Here are some pros and cons to consider for both platonic and romantic office relationships:

Pros to a Platonic Office Relationship: The saying "it takes a village" can apply to having platonic office relationships, too, as most people's work is interdependent. Everyone you meet has something to offer, whether they are a teacher, friend, strong ally, or business colleague. You can never have too many friends, or at least acquaintances! Sometimes, the relationship continues after your office time together ends, and sometimes it does not. Either is fine. Having a solid platonic relationship can benefit each party.

Cons to a Platonic Office Relationship: Investing time in any relationships of any type may not pay off. People can misinterpret words or actions as romantic intentions when they are not. Relationships can ebb and flow, and sometimes, if they fall into a negative flow, you might not want to maintain the relationship, even when you might have to in a professional scenario.

Office relationships are potential disasters. Most people should not take the risk of pursuing romantic partners. If the relationship does not work out, consider how difficult it might be for each of you to professionally carry on in your respective roles.

Pros to an Office Romance: There is a chance this relationship could turn out to be a solid one that becomes serious enough to take it to a different level than anticipated. However, navigating through the emotional roller coaster you will be on might make it awkward for your colleagues. If you happen to work at a large company, and you rarely see or interact with one another, this could be a pro reason to pursue your relationship.

Cons to an Office Romance: It is really difficult to mitigate the dangers associated with a romantic office relationship. You might think you are being discreet, but more people than you think will pick up on the romantic vibe. Depending on your role, there could be an enormous conflict of interest. Emotions are difficult to mask, especially when you are upset by a partner. This can be exacerbated when the person you are having negative emotions with is in your working environment.

Having an office relationship can place unwarranted judgement on your decision-making abilities. Don't let this happen to you.

| Harnessing Your Leadership Skills |

What would this world be like if we did not have leaders? One thing I can attest to is that there is a tremendous difference between good and great leaders. Do you work for a great leader, or are you one? Or, are you one in the making?

Leadership is not for everyone. Even some people who are in leadership positions do not belong in the role. Having worked for numerous leaders during the course of my 25 years in business, I have witnessed a wide array of leadership types and levels of competency. But I have learned from both the amazing and not-so-great leaders. And I discerned that amazing leaders share a number of similar traits.

During my professional marketing career, I worked at a combination of both start-up and well-established companies. The start-up business leaders taught me the most about leadership. Their multi-faceted skills were what enabled them to navigate and grow their companies in the face of continuous high risk, especially during hyper growth or unknown growth periods when a new product or service was being launched.

In my opinion, the number one skill each of these leaders possessed was their high level of emotional intelligence, or EQ. To the best of my knowledge, this is not a skill that is taught in business school, but is purely an innate talent. When someone has a high degree of EQ, this does not guarantee they will be a successful leader, but the best ones I worked for leveraged this skill every day in highly demonstrable ways.

Some of the ways the highly successful leaders leveraged their EQ was by being able to easily read people and know how to motivate them. They were also able to get along well with people, regardless of the role they played in the organization. Possessing the ability to provide a crystal-clear vision, in both verbal and written communications, of where and how a company will achieve its goals, is also an essential skill the best leaders I worked for possessed.

The majority of the best leaders also exuded charisma, and were very likeable people. They also earned your respect, and you wanted to follow and do your best work for them. The majority of them were demanding and had extremely high standards across the board, but they were also fair and non-judgmental. Being open minded was an attribute they all possessed, too.

Ironically, not all of the people who I would classify as a leader were in fact leaders. However, they possessed the characteristics and traits associated with successful leaders, and were clearly heading towards being one at some point in their career.

A recent non-business example of a person who is destined to be a leader is a young man I recently worked with who was on a sports team that I mentored as a performance and motivation coach. He'd be the first person to tell you he was probably the least-talented player on the team from a field skill perspective. But that didn't matter, as his role on the team was more important on the sidelines and in the locker room. He exhibited all of the characteristics of a leader in the making, and his teammates recognized this at the end of the season by naming him to be one of the captains of the team during his senior year.

If you think you are a leader in the making, wish to be one someday, or are already a leader, you are performing one of the most important roles you will play in your professional life. I encourage you to model your leadership style after well-known leaders regardless of their industry. Don't delay cultivating your leadership skills, as you are doing a disservice to yourself and to those you are leading when you do not possess the right or essential leadership skills.

How will you know if you are a great leader? Chances are you have been told you are; but if you have not regularly heard that you are, then you might have some more work to do to get that great leader designation.

‖ Discovering Your Motivation ‖

Inspiration can come from many places and in many different forms that can propel people to new levels of success they did not believe possible. Knowing how to discover what motivates you is the key to being happy and successful in your career. Have you established your motivation factors?

Similar to a person's palm and the lines on it, no two people have exactly the same motivators. This is good, because if we were all motivated by the same things, our world would not be nearly as interesting and diverse. When was the last time you paused to think about what motivates you, or have you already figured it out?

Traveling and meeting new people motivates me. I am always honored to become acquainted with total strangers. After speaking with them, whether it's 10 minutes or a few hours, I have a new understanding of the person I first met.

I am not a huge fan of watching the news, as it only gives you the perspective from the people who are editing the information you see. I would much rather conduct my own interviews and do my own analysis on current events. Ideally, this would be done by having conversations with people who live in different parts of the world.

Not everyone is self-motivated, so fortunately there are other people, places, and things that can provide inspiration. If you decide to get in shape and want to go the gym, but have no idea how to use the equipment, hiring a personal trainer to help you makes perfect sense. The process and planning itself can help motivate you to become fit.

Likewise, if you want to become better at something professionally, you can seek out someone who has already mastered the task. The mentor or master can serve as the motivation, while simultaneously teaching you how to improve performance.

Many people are inspired by sports stars or business icons, or potentially by a youth coach dedicated to helping kids learn how to play a sport.

Valuable lessons are associated with competitive-level sports. Inspiration can also come from admiring what other people have achieved from a professional perspective whether they are in a traditional role, such as a surgeon, or perhaps an opera singer.

Inspiration can also come from nature, such as admiring the work of the father of American landscape architecture Frederick Law Olmsted who, with his senior partner Calvert Vaux, designed New York City's Central Park, Boston's Emerald Necklace, and San Francisco's Golden Gate Park.

Still not sure what motivates you? Here are some questions to ask yourself:

1| Is there something I enjoy doing that inspires me? Is there a way to monetize my passion?

2| What are two or three possibilities I regularly think about when I am not doing the work I get paid to do?

3| Is there something in my life with which I have never lost interest? Is it something I never tire of, and which also brings me joy when I do it (playing golf, painting pictures, playing an instrument, coaching a team or volunteering time to tutor others)?

4| What do I daydream about when I am at work? What's an activity I wish I were doing instead of working where I am now?

5| What is something I would do for which I would gladly sacrifice sleep or money?

6| What do I enjoy doing — something that increases my energy, puts a spring in my step, and brings a smile to my face?

Answer the questions above and then study your responses. You may notice a pattern of things you like to do, and activities that can serve as motivators. They will inspire you to do more of the things you want.

Motivation can come from within or from others or things around you. Your assignment is to figure out which one or a combination of these are what motivates you to have a better career and life. It's inspiring!

|| When People Get Quiet ||

Have you ever noticed when the office vibe is more subdued than usual? Or perhaps you get a feeling something is different, but you cannot put your finger on exactly what has changed? A quiet office typically signals something is going on. Are you perceptive enough to pick up on this, and take advantage of discovering the reason?

Call it your gut or intuition, but there is definitely a sense you feel when something is not quite right. At work, it's often related to either a promotion, a firing, or rumors that the company is being acquired by another firm. Some might consider this sensibility akin to a psychic power, but whatever you call it, I believe everyone has this ability. Most, however, might not know how to tap into it. Having this skill can be both helpful and stressful, as it acts as a barometer of the pressure being felt in the office.

There is a saying, "The calm before the storm." I have felt this more than I care to admit. Most of the time, something good is about to happen, but people are not allowed to talk about it, so they tend to get quiet, or act more reserved than normal. Conversely, when something ominous is about to occur, this same sense of quiet tends to permeate the building, almost like a fog. Generally, just a few people in the office set this tone, and may not even be aware of what they are doing. However, there are signs you can watch for to determine if something different is about to occur.

- The people who have the inside scoop, whether it is positive or negative, will generally start to avoid eye contact prior to the reveal. Those in the know will have a slightly different demeanor than normal. If they are usually talkative, they may become quiet, or vice versa.

- When asked questions that might either be on target or are close to what might be going on, the person who knows may get fidgety and exhibit signs of being nervous (e.g., their neck turns red, they may start to sweat slightly on their forehead). Or the response to your questions, which would normally be longer, will be short, curt, and maybe even abrupt.

If you encounter any of these behaviors from the people who know something, try not to pressure them into telling you anything. They generally are not in a position to do so. Later, they will thank you for your patience and respect. Depending on how well you know them, and what type of relationship you have developed, they may offer hints about what is going on, and whether it is positive or negative.

People in new leadership roles, and who may not have years of experience with change management, will be much more transparent and easier to read than those with years of experience. Of course, this is a generalization, but more often than not, newer managers will have a more difficult time not displaying their emotions. This is not a bad thing. It is part of how you learn. With practice, next time you will do a better job of not revealing any secrets through your facial expressions or body language.

Being able to read what is going on and tapping into the sense that allows you to do this, can help to prepare you for what is likely about to happen. We're not talking about a self-fulfilling prophesy, but instead thinking through your options. It is far better to be aware than caught off guard when something potentially disastrous happens. Being too emotional in most office settings is not generally considered an asset. Master the ability to control your emotions — composed on the outside even though you might be a hot mess inside.

Most managers and upper level executives become quite good at masking their emotions, but being able to read the cues they are giving off will serve you well. Learn from the best so that in future sticky situations, when you need to be composed and thinking clearly, you will be!

|| Banishing Harassment ||

This is one of the most personal articles I have written, and one that has taken awhile to even consider writing. But I know that writing can be therapeutic, and can serve others as well, so this is for those who have been suffering in silence; or who have been the target of any type of harassment. When a victim speaks out, please listen, and offer support any way you can. No one should have to contend with having been harassed under any circumstances, especially in the workplace.

Recently, there has been an abundance of reports of sexual harassment incidents, and both sexes have come out to tell their stories. More women than men have come forward with allegations of having been harassed in the workplace, and it appears we have reached a tipping point in terms of victims finally being heard in the mainstream media.

Unfortunately, many victims of harassment have suffered in silence for years, and when they have come forward, they have often been met with resistance or even disbelief. Many were told it might not be worth the effort to pursue legal or any consequential action.

Having worked the majority of my career in a male-dominated field, I have both witnessed and been a victim of harassment. I have had to report harassment charges for others and for myself, and I can assure you, I was incredibly dissatisfied with how the scenarios were handled.

Disgust and disappointment are a few of the polite words I use to express how I feel about the experiences. As both a victim and reporter of harassment, I can state I never want any one of my children to experience this seemingly epidemic behavior. This is part of the reason why I'm speaking out.

At the beginning of each year, I would literally think, "perhaps this is the year the harassment will stop." But it is only after being in the workforce for more than 25 years, that I am finally hopeful that harassment might be something with which we no longer have to contend. So I have a renewed sense of optimism that we are heading towards it not being tolerated under any circumstances.

This topic needs to remain front and center, and there must be severe consequences for those who harass others.

We also need to make it easier and safe for victims to report harassment, and not be blamed for being a "snitch." Indeed, I have felt unsafe, and as if I were being targeted for reporting harassment. This should never be something anyone should have to deal with, and by coming out and publicly revealing my own experience on this topic, I hope I can give strength to others who wish to do the same.

As you have noticed, I have not revealed the names of the people who harassed me. They know who they are. Nor have I revealed the names of the people I have had to report who harassed others. Being both a victim and an abuse reporter are not activities I ever dreamed I would have to deal with professionally.

Looking forward, if I were to be granted a wish for the future, it is that this is the year we start to see a significant decrease in the amount of harassment, leading quickly towards this type of behavior as something that my children and others in the workforce do not ever have to think about.

|| Identifying Your Process Personality ||

A few years ago, I started thinking about what part of work I enjoy the most, and concluded that I adore the beginning of projects, major events, small meetings — the planning stages. One of my strengths is that I think strategically. There is just something about having to plan what needs to happen to get started that really motivates me. Do you have a starter personality, or do you prefer the middle process or finishing the assignment?

My sister and I always joke around about how similar, yet different, we are. One of the common traits we share is our fondness for starting things. I come from a family of entrepreneurs, so perhaps this characteristic is simply hard-wired into our DNA. Although I love the process of beginning things, this does not mean I am keen on the rest of the process — the middle and the end.

I am absolutely capable of starting and finishing projects, but realize my gift is in being the catalyst. Fortunately, I have learned to surround myself with colleagues or team members who enjoy the middle and end parts.

If you had to classify which part of a process you gravitate to the most, is there one you particularly enjoy more than the others? Or, are you the type of person who enjoys the entire journey? There are different skill sets required for each of the three parts of accomplishing tasks. Knowing which category you are most closely aligned with should help you better navigate your career choices.

Starters are creative, visionary, strategic, and organized. They are able to explain the *why* behind the project. In addition, Starters are:
- Process-oriented;
- Have strong negotiation skills;
- Offer exceptional communication skills; and
- Have mastered the art of "selling their concepts."

A few traits of Middles include a strong motivation to not let the team down. They enjoy the process of working on or honing a task in progress. They are reliable and detail-oriented.

In addition, Middles have:
- Advanced project management skills;
- Strong problem-solving skills; and
- An acceptance of working behind the scenes, not in the spotlight.

Finishers are disciplined, resourceful, and dependable. They are strong at processing information required to complete the project, and can envision the finish line because they know what it will take to accomplish the work. Finishers are also:
- Fierce negotiators;
- Spurred by a thrill from seeing the project through to completion; and
- Enjoy the spotlight, especially when the project is being debuted.

Based on the breakdown above, do you now see yourself differently? Will you now consider taking on different types of projects or trying to find a role that is more suited to your strengths?

When you are able to apply your strengths regularly, you will be much more satisfied with the work you are doing and the people with whom you are working. You might even view your company in a different, more optimistic light. Your positive attitude will likely be enhanced as well.

When people come into the proper alignment with the part of a process they most enjoy, everyone wins!

|| Building a Strong Team ||

Not everyone will have an opportunity to build a team, but if you hope to one day, or if you are already building and developing teams, there are always new strategies to learn and implement.

Many factors will contribute to how successful a team will be. One of these success factors has to do with who you had the privilege of being mentored by as you were coming up the ranks. If you were led by an emotionally intelligent and common-sense oriented boss/mentor, consider yourself fortunate. If your boss/mentor also had mastered being empathetic, and was able to coach you through tough business scenarios, consider yourself to be in an elite group of managers.

What if your former bosses were not skilled people or motivational leaders? How do you learn these skills to build and develop exceptional, high-performing teams? One way is to identify a manager within your organization whom you or others admire for their management qualities. Ask them if you can meet with them weekly for 30 minutes to learn from them. Assuming they say yes, be sure to have questions to ask, and a well-planned agenda. Ideally, share your agenda with your chosen mentor prior to the meeting to give them time to prepare for the meeting.

You can also ask to shadow them, after you have built up enough time with them to move to this level of leadership mentoring. Depending on the size of your company, find out if there is a management training track available.

Some companies see the value of having a management rotation process in place. If your company offers this training, find out how you can participate.

For those of you who are already leading a team, how do you know you have the right team in place? For those of you who have adopted teams to manage, you still have an opportunity to treat the team as if you are building it out from scratch. The best way to accomplish this is to take your team offsite, ideally for two days. During your offsite, let the members know you want to re-establish the team as if it were new, and that you want to get everyone on board.

As a Certified Gallup StrengthsFinder Coach, I would be remiss if I didn't suggest you check out leveraging *Strengths Finder 2.0* by Tom Rath, who explains how to deploy a concept of identifying each team member's top five strengths as the basis for doing a team reset. A StrengthsFinder Coach can also be invaluable in leading your team development. Alternately, assign a facilitator to take you through the strengths exercises. This will give team members a new way to get to know each other and will reset their understanding of how to ideally leverage each member's strengths.

If you are in a position to hire a team from scratch, review these six high-level guidelines for helping you to hire the right people.

1| Ensure the person you are bringing onto your team fits your corporate and team culture.

2| Have everyone on the team interview the candidate. Coordinate interview questions to avoid wasting your team and the candidate's time. Debrief with your team after the interviews are completed.

3| Input candidate feedback into an online system if your company has one, or improvise and provide team members with a score card. Since some interview processes can last weeks, being able to refer back to interview feedback will be helpful. If the vote to hire the person is not unanimous, then reject the candidate. Developing a hiring consensus is one of the best ways to accelerate the on-boarding process for a new team member.

4| Check the candidate's references. Ask tough questions. You might be surprised by what you learn — both good and bad.

5| If possible, ask the candidate to shadow your team for half a day. You and the candidate will learn much more about each other this way, and it will give each of you an opportunity to "test drive" a potential working relationship.

6| Trust your gut. Even if the person looks perfect on paper and interviews like a pro, if your gut tells you there is something not right about this candidate, trust your instincts, as they are often spot on accurate.

Chapter 2 | Life

|| Believe In Yourself ||

The longer I am on this planet, the more I embrace the idea of how just about everything works out the way it is supposed to. When you were young, you might have heard this phrase spoken by adults, and like me, thought, "That sounds way too optimistic, and not at all comforting." But as I aged, I began to embrace this concept, and let go of some control. What happened? It was as if circumstances and situations actually worked out better than expected. That's the secret of positivity.

Have you ever found yourself in the middle of a situation that does not appear to be going in the right direction and thought, "How is this possibly going to work out?"

Or, perhaps you have had more than your fair share of good luck. Either way, most of us have had challenges in both life and business scenarios with which to contend. For some, it seems as if there's no favorable conclusion. But then, lo and behold, the outcome is far better than expected.

So many people spend an enormous amount of energy worrying about factors they cannot control, or consequences that are unlikely to happen. I have a hard time relating to this, as I try my best to do the opposite, and guess what? Things usually turn out better than I anticipated. Sometimes fabulously so.

In the meantime, I do not expend any energy concerning myself with factors I cannot control or that will not realistically happen. For example, I'm pretty sure nobody will actually faint from nerves in the middle of a presentation. Of course, there is that self-fulfilling prophecy thing, but I prefer not to succumb to the negative, and think about what good things could happen instead.

When you adopt the approach of spending less time worrying about negative consequences, you free yourself to apply your energy to much more productive work or activities. This is a far more desirable approach. Once you begin to implement this concept, you will start to see more positive outcomes from this paradigm mind shift.

Visualization is a technique that can be practiced along with more optimistic thinking. Using visualization simply requires you to close your eyes and imagine that what is worrying you will have a positive outcome. Many athletes and business executives leverage this, and agree it is enormously helpful. When you are able to envision a positive outcome of what you are attempting *before* it happens, you are essentially practicing how to succeed.

Another concept, *The Secret*, has proven successful for many, including myself, to provoking a desired outcome. Simply put, I am always amazed by the results. *The Secret* concept purports to essentially leverage powers you were not aware of, but that you have to work with. I have coached people on how to leverage the concept, and 100% of the time the outcomes have surpassed expectations. The trick is to allow your mind to be open to the concept, and then let go of worry and anxiety to allow the power of this concept to work for you.

Imagine an hour, half a day, or even weeks of not worrying about whether [fill-in-the-blank] is going to work out. How would your life be different if you thought this way? What if you had more energy to invest into improving your life or career? I know you can embrace at least one or several of these concepts. Trust and believe that in the end, everything will work out the way it is supposed to. Even being fired could lead to a whole new, better-paying, more satisfying career. It could happen!

| Turn It Off |

When was the last time you turned off all of your electronic gadgets and totally unplugged from the world? Last week? Last month? Never? Being able to totally unplug is a pleasure — and a gift.

Don't think you are up to the challenge? What if you tried it for 30 minutes today? What would you do with the extra time? The ultimate challenge is to detach for an entire day. Can you imagine what might happen? I experimented with doing this for two weeks, and here is what happened.

Being on the other side of the world makes one think differently. Or at least it did me. Part of this had to do with the fact that I was traveling alone, and had extremely limited access to the typical electronic communications gadgets I am accustomed to using. This was simultaneously nerve wracking and liberating. The stressful part had more to do with always feeling like I have to be plugged into the pulse of the world. The liberation came from being able to ignore what is going on — at least for a period of time. Being 15 hours ahead of most of my family and friends also presented some rather interesting challenges and outcomes. They were all worth it.

One of the best results of limited access to world events is that it forced me to ask others, to pick up a newspaper, or simply not be informed. When you are able to unplug from the day-to-day distractions life offers, you are more willing to consider doing things you might not normally do. One is to get out and talk to people. Yes, actually strike up a conversation and perhaps meet a future friend. The fact I was traveling alone and had years of practice of doing this made it a bit easier for me to be comfortable with this tactic. The truth is, I find it refreshing.

During my trip, I was essentially unplugged for more hours than I am typically. During this down time, I had the opportunity to do new things, see some sights, and meet people I never would have met had I been tethered to my gadgets and Wi-Fi connection.

One new friend was building a development on one of the Fiji Islands. He had been patiently waiting for five years for his paperwork to be approved so he could start the actual building process. He is now in the early construction phase, and anticipates opening his resort late next year. I never would have connected with this man if I had not met and agreed to have dinner with two people I became friends with earlier in the week.

When you take the time to unplug from the rest of the world, it also changes how your mind starts to process information. You begin to think through scenarios with an entirely new level of clarity and detail. This happens because you are not constantly distracted by all of the interruptions that either you allow to enter into your thought process by perhaps a simple "click" on a link, or because you switch between your gadgets to see what they might offer you from an information perspective.

Sometimes people tell me they are becoming less able to concentrate and potentially feel like they might have attention deficit issues. It's their gadgets, frankly. When you allow yourself to get away from them, you become amazed at how your concentration levels improve.

Some people are too quick to depend on medication to help them to have better focus, and we know the medication only provides a temporary solution. Yes, it's my opinion, but who really wants to take more medication? Aggh, "no one" is the answer, contrary to what the pharmaceutical companies want you to believe. The good news is that there is a potentially and more simple, non-pharmaceutical solution.

Are you ready to take on the challenge of unplugging?

Perhaps it will require some planning, but the results could be worth the effort. Don't deny yourself the opportunity to experience a whole new world — if only for 30 minutes, or half a day. . . or a week. Just think of the possibilities!

‖ Don't Look Back ‖

Looking in the proverbial rear view mirror can be insightful, but it is easier, and safer, to keep your eyes and mind on the road ahead. Dealing with what happened in the past, or living in the past, is not going to do you any favors. Having things to look forward to is a much healthier way to think and live.

I cannot speak for anyone else, but one of the things that really motivates me is looking forward to something. Even when there is not anything monumental on the horizon, I look forward to something as simple as sharing a cup of coffee with a friend. Having something to anticipate is simple enough to accomplish — and a highly achievable experience!

It's normal for all of us to reminisce about past accomplishments, joyous experiences, or even some less-than-ideal days; but dwelling on the past should not consume your thoughts. "What if" thinking serves little purpose, consumes too much energy, and is a habit we are all guilty of and one we should try to break. Instead, let's take this thinking and apply it towards the future.

When we interrupt negative thinking, we do ourselves and others a favor by changing our attitudes towards just about everything. Thinking in terms of possibilities versus reviewing our playback tape is what highly successful and motivated people do. It really is not that difficult.

The first challenge is to recognize a pattern of thinking about what has already happened, especially since you cannot rewrite what has already occurred. The good news is that you do have control over the script for what can happen next.

Stop and really think about this for a minute. Yes, you do have full control. Don't *let* it happen, *make* it happen!

Use one of these five tips to refocus your energy and attention on looking ahead instead of in the rear-view mirror.

1| Think of someone you admire. Now imagine yourself in their shoes. What are their most admirable characteristics? Are some of their traits ones that you could borrow and implement?

2| Spend time outside. Being near or around nature, or simply breathing in fresh air, can reset your thinking and put you in a better, more positive frame of mind.

3| Do something nice for someone else. Thinking through the process of doing a kind gesture for someone else forces you to think ahead and plan out the activity, even when it is a simple action like putting a blanket on your child or significant other when he or she has fallen asleep on the couch.

4| Put together a plan. It can be almost any kind of plan — a vacation, dinner date, birthday party, etc. The simple act of starting a plan will create the need to look forward.

5| Get out of your routine. No matter what time of the day it is, you probably have a routine. Do something entirely different during your day, and start thinking now what it might be. This will give you something to look forward to, and put you in a position to have to think about doing something later.

Changing how you think about the future can create positive results. The natural endorphins released from the brain when you are thinking and doing constructive behavior will help.

I know you can do this, and promise it's worth the effort. I have coached many people who felt the same way you do, and guided them to be able to do this well, and every day. Give it a try.

| Stop Criticizing Others |

Without realizing it, some people come across as critical of others. They provide unsolicited commentary, which is typically negative and unwelcome. This is a bad habit that should be broken. Are you guilty?

People who criticize are typically insecure and because of this, focus their attention on others instead of being reflective. When you come across someone like this, steer the other way. Who wants to be around a Debbie or David Downer? No one! If you spend too much time with them, others might think you are this way, too. But what if you are the one who is overly critical of others? Do you even realize it?

Let's take a virtual walk around your office and come up with some scenarios of interactions you might have. The first takes place shortly after you have arrived at work. You exchange pleasantries with others, or so you think. You may not have realized you offered negative commentary during an interaction with one of your colleagues when she told you how she spent her weekend. Did you need to be judgmental about your colleague's choices and then share your opinion? No, you did not.

In the next scenario, you're talking with a colleague following a meeting you both attended. Instead of providing constructive feedback, you criticized the presenter for how she delivered the information, and groused about how you did not like the format.

Another interaction typical of Negative Neds or Nellies is during a break from work, such as a short, refreshing walk around the building after lunch. These quick breaks offer opportunities for upbeat conversations with colleagues. But, if you are an overly critical person, you tend to use this interaction to complain. Does this sound like you, or someone you know?

If you are the person who is critical of others and have yet to realize it, there are ways to determine if you are guilty, and to course correct your behavior. Consider the interactions you have had the last few days. After the encounter, did you feel better, neutral, or worse? If you felt better or neutral, was there a positive outcome, or did you simply feel relieved about sharing your opinion?

If you had to grade your conversations with others as if you were rating a restaurant on Yelp, how many stars would you give yourself, and why? Are there situations or people who trigger your critical nature? Begin to recognize whether these happen routinely, or only periodically.

Here are additional tips on how to stop being overly critical of others:

1| Jot down positive things you can share and say about others, then sprinkle these expressions into your conversations. Did they react differently?

2| Create a list of typical topics you chat about with others. What percentage are critical versus constructive or positive? Do this exercise for one week to work towards changing the types of exchanges you have been having.

3| Ask a friend if they think you have tendencies to be critical of others. If they are a true friend, they will be candid with you. Do not be mad at them for being honest with you, and instead, thank them for their assessment.

4| Challenge yourself to work towards being a less critical person, and check your progress from week to week to see if you are decreasing your negative commentary about others or situations.

No one sets out to be critical of others. Sometimes behaving this way is a result of picking up bad behavior from observing others who might be doing the same thing. Some critical people believe they are only "helping" others by pointing out flaws. Might that resonate with you? The trick to becoming less critical and ultimately more fun to be around, is to acknowledge you might be this way, and then to work towards overcoming this bad habit.

Once you become less critical of others, you will become a happier person and others will take notice.

‖ The Comparison Game ‖

It's human nature to compare ourselves to others, but is it really of any value? Wouldn't you be better off if you stopped comparing yourself to others and instead focused on what you want to do? What can happen when you set yourself free from comparison?

Most of us are guilty of comparing ourselves to others, and sometimes this can be helpful, assuming we do so in a constructive manner. However, most people compare themselves to others and find deficits that discourage them. What if you stopped comparing yourself to others and instead developed goals for yourself to achieve — ones that are reasonable and obtainable?

And often the comparisons we think others are making of us are simply not true. (And anyway, what other people think of us is none of our business.) The perceived deficiencies we claim as our own are self-defeating. Given the choice, I am certain you would rather feel uplifted than defeated any day.

Ready to change? Stop comparing yourself to anyone else, in any manner. This will not be easy, as society constantly places pressure on us to contrast and compare. Deciding to be free from comparisons is something that is achievable, and a great goal to have.

During a recent conversation with a colleague, he spoke about how his sister never participated in sports, and does not fully understand or appreciate the value of being focused on regular exercise. His teenaged nephew had been offered an opportunity to receive professional personal training, something that would help the teen in his recent attempts to get in shape. The frustrated uncle admitted to me that he was comparing his nephew, who has enormous athletic potential, to other kids his age, yet does not want to work to develop his potential. This young man's mother has not been supportive of her son's interest in getting in better physical shape, and, in fact, has had discouraging conversations with her brother about helping her son. However, her brother is not yet ready to give up on his nephew.

The best part of the conversation was that my colleague was able to recognize that he was unfairly comparing his interest in being in good physical shape, with his sister, who has no experience or interest in the subject. He told me that she criticized him for his interest in and knowledge of physical fitness, and said that it was ridiculous. He acknowledged that it was ridiculous because she does not understand the topic. He noted that it would be similar to him speaking with her about how to be a makeup expert, which he clearly is not.

The fact this man was able to recognize the importance of not comparing his knowledge with his sister's is critical. This will allow him to remain open to eventually support and guide his nephew if and when the young man is ready to accept help.

We also discussed comparing his nephew to other boys his age. This is perfectly normal to do, and in this instance, he claimed that his goal was to bolster the reason he wanted to help his nephew.

In the grand scheme of things, his nephew's physical level should not matter, especially if the young man himself is not concerned with being compared to others his age from a physical fitness perspective.

This conversation illustrates how others place judgments on us, and how we accept, deny, or go to a neutral place of thinking about the comparison being made, and what is really important.

Since the nephew is young, he is likely influenced by comparisons. In this case, the one being made is constructive, and intended to help. This could make a difference in how it is received. Or not.

We can all do without negative comparisons. The next time you think about comparing yourself to someone else in any manner, ask yourself why, and whether the conclusions hold any truth or are at all helpful. My guess is the comparison you are making is less than constructive.

Instead, why not think about a positive aspect of your life, as I am sure you have a number of them.

‖ 10 Reasons Why You Should Be Daydreaming ‖

Were you ever called out in school for daydreaming? Yes, you probably should have been paying attention to the lesson being presented, but it is possible that what you were daydreaming about was actually the foundation for your future. Instead of being taught that daydreaming is a negative activity, it should be embraced as something more people, at any age, should try. Imagine how many of the inventions and advancements we enjoy today may not have been created without someone first daydreaming. Are you a daydream believer?

When was the last time you caught yourself daydreaming? This is something I find myself doing regularly. It often serves as inspiration for the work I do. Daydreaming can even be helpful in solving challenges — an extension of the thinking-through process. Some might refer to the act of daydreaming in other expressive ways. This concept serves multiple purposes and results in more positive than negative outcomes.

No one would argue that time is one of our most precious resources, but they might tell you daydreaming is not a productive use of time. I disagree.

Let's imagine if people did not daydream. Would they be more productive, happier, healthier, and ultimately more satisfied with their life? Probably not. Daydreaming is a form of natural therapy which can calm anxiety and provide hope and inspiration to achieve what once seemed impossible.

I have found that when daydreaming, I am, in fact, architecting in my mind the potential outcome. I use daydreaming to help me think through conundrums either for myself, my clients, friends, or family. Since most of us do not remember our overnight dreams, I am thankful we can remember our daydreams. We can leverage them to transport us to places we might not otherwise be able to go for any number of reasons — health, mobility issues, finances, or fear.

Do you daydream? If not, why not? Is it because you think it is a waste of time? Is it because you do not have anything you think is worthy of daydreaming about? Or, does the possibility of seeing yourself in a better place seem too scary?

Regardless of which camp you find yourself, rethink daydreaming with this daydreaming rationale.

1| Daydreaming can be like taking a mini mental vacation each and every day.

2| Daydreaming can encourage you to do more than you think you can.

3| Daydreaming allows you to place (or imagine) yourself in different scenarios and can help you to prepare to step up or in when the actual time comes. It is similar to the concept of visualization.

4| Daydreaming can provide your mind and body with a way to decrease stress by thinking about things that are more positive.

5| Creative minds need time to relax and capture mental power from various sources. Daydreaming is often a source that fuels those with creative minds.

6| Inspiration can come from daydreaming, which in turn allows you to continue, pursue, or embark upon something you want to achieve.

7| Numerous inventions have been inspired by daydreaming as the catalyst for the idea to come to fruition.

8| Problem solvers will often apply the act of daydreaming to help their minds switch gears and develop methods and solutions.

9| Healing can take place when our minds have an opportunity to check-out from reality and go to a happier place, which in turn can release natural healing chemicals in our brains.

10| Those who are dealing with physical or mental issues can use daydreaming to help them see themselves in a better and more positive situation than the one they are currently in.

In other words, daydreaming can offer people hope on days it may be in short supply. Since daydreaming is free and easy to do, why not give it a try for a week or two? See if you change your mind or reinforce your beliefs about the benefits of this practice.

| Why Are You So Unhappy? |

Who doesn't want to be happy? I ask myself this question when I come across people who seem to ooze negativity. We have all encountered these people. Mental health could certainly play a role; but do some people simply choose to be unhappy?

My mother is wise woman. One of the things she has routinely conveyed to me is the philosophy that you always have a choice. You can choose to be happy. I am not sure why someone would choose to *not* be happy, but I know such people exist. I have had to work with a number of them. I am sure you have, too, but is there something you can do to help these Debbie Downers, and is it worth doing? I think it is!

Although many of us come into this world crying, we did so for physiological reasons — to take oxygen into our lungs to breathe. When we see babies, we typically smile, and, as we all know, smiling is contagious. Scientific studies show that even if you force a smile, you can trick your psyche into thinking you are happier.

Since smiling is an easy thing to do, and since it is contagious, when someone else smiles at us we will generally mimic this expression. Most people look friendlier and more approachable when they smile. Although some smiles can look a bit intimidating and disingenuous, they are easy to identify. Even a fake smile is preferable to a scowl.

Mental health issues are a serious problem in our country. Often those suffering take their challenges to work, where their colleagues have to contend with mental health issues not being managed properly. Loneliness has also become one of the more recent manifestations people of all ages contend with in this age of digital interactions. It is both a social and psychological phenomenon, and has been linked partially to depression.

Even though most people are not mental health experts, and helping someone with such challenges should be left to a professional, there are things you can do to help. Sometimes simply offering to talk to them if they seem open to conversation can help. But how do you recognize the symptoms of someone who is lonely or depressed? One company based in

New York City, Kognito, helps tackle this problem with guided, game-based simulations and other technology resources. They focus on helping those without professional mental health training on how to help people who are at risk for having a serious mental health event.

There are various levels of happiness and it is not possible to be happy 100% of the time. It would be a wonderful challenge to undertake to see how close we could get to full happiness. In all seriousness, happiness is partly a mental as well as a physical state. If we do not feel well either mentally or physically, it is harder to feel happy.

Conversely, when we feel well, take good care of ourselves, and our minds are in a healthy state, happiness is much easier to experience. So, why do people with whom we work who are perceived to be healthy and in mentally good shape come across as unhappy?

When I have coached and mentored employees who present themselves negatively, quite often they do not realize they are projecting their unhappiness. They actually think they are doing a great job of masking their feelings, and that no one can tell they are miserable. To address this, I bring a mirror to the meeting and ask them to literally make the various expressions they would typically make while interacting with their colleagues. When they see their facial expressions reflected in the mirror, most of them are shocked. Once they are aware of how their emotions are being conveyed, we work on modifying their facial expressions to reflect what they want to project. You can do this same exercise with a friend, or even a trusted colleague.

It bears repeating — everyone deserves to be happy! Choosing to be happy is something most people would say they would prefer. One quick test you can do to determine if others' perception matches what you are thinking is to ask them to rate, on a scale of one to five (with five being the happiest) how they perceive your happiness level. Ultimately, being happy and the level of which happiness number you achieve is up to you, but you can definitely become happier than you are.

‖ Prove Them Wrong ‖

Have you ever had someone tell you that you can't accomplish a goal? Did it make you stop pursuing what you wanted, or did it fuel your passion to pursue your desire? I hope, for your sake, it was the latter choice, and if it wasn't, I truly wish that you have an opportunity to someday experience this. I have. It's like rocket fuel.

I will never forget the emotions that swept over me when my high school guidance counselor told me I probably should not consider college. His advice was based on the scores of my SAT test. According to his chart, they were not high enough for me to be attractive to a college. What he did not factor in were my grades, which were outstanding, and my drive as a highly competitive athlete. I never paid attention to anyone who told me I could not do something I wanted to do. If I had to think of a word that fueled my desire to pursue a college degree, it would be *confidence.*

My confidence was built on the athletic field. I felt invincible when I was out there playing. The better I became athletically, the more confidence it gave me academically. However, my grades and standardized test scores were not in alignment. The guidance counselor had not considered me as a whole person, but instead as just someone with two numbers that could determine my higher education options.

When he told me he did not think I would be able to go to college, it ignited a competitive fire — and he struck the match. He had no idea!

What resulted from my athletic competitiveness was the attention of just about every major Ivy League and highly-recognized soccer and lacrosse program in the country. It's a long story, but I did not end up pursuing my options to compete at the college level. However, I proved the guidance counselor wrong by having the results of my academic and sports abilities override the importance of the SAT numbers. Do I regret not playing? No, as it was more satisfying to get into a college on my own terms, and prove the naysayer wrong.

Have you ever really wanted to do or be something, but either had perceived obstacles prevent you from obtaining what you were going after, or actual obstacles that made it difficult to achieve your goal? Were you frustrated enough to stop pursuing your goal, or did it set in motion the energy and passion you needed?

If you have run into obstacles, here are some ideas to help clear the path. There is always more than one solution to any problem or challenge. Keep looking. I promise you will find them.

- Don't give up. Even if you think, deep in the recesses of your normally positive mind, that there is no possibility, keep at it. Think of how many times author J.K. Rowling of the Harry Potter series was rejected by publishers before one took her on as a client (about a dozen)!

- Tap into your network, or your network's network, to enlist the support of people willing to donate their time, expertise, and encouragement to help you reach your goal. Sometimes, people just need to be asked, and, more often than you might think, they will say *yes*.

- Build a support system of people who will encourage your goals, and be there for you on both the good, and particularly on the rough, days.

- Keep your eyes on the prize. What does it look like? What will it feel like when you get there? What will be different when you conquer the challenge?

There is great satisfaction proving someone wrong, provided it is not done in a spiteful way. I hope you have the chance to have the same empowering feeling I have had, more than once.

It's corny, but it's true. When you believe, you can achieve. Now go do it!

‖ Who Is My Example? ‖

When I assess today's leaders to see if there is someone I would like to be like — someone who works professionally to motivate and inspire people, the only person who comes to my mind is Tony Robbins. But, I am not even slightly like him. And when I try to think of the equivalent female version of him, I can't think of anyone. So . . . could it be me?

Never did I dream I would be thinking, let alone writing, about my thoughts and dreams. All of my writing has been directly sourced from the person most of you have never seen or met. I only recently revealed to a dear friend something I always wanted to do, but did not pursue due to my dyslexia — acting. So, what did I do instead? The obvious next thing was to become a marketing executive!

All kidding aside, I am certain many people have something they wanted to pursue and did not. It might not be too late for me to alter my desire and instead pursue something similar to acting. I can — I will — become an inspirational and motivational speaker.

The reason I want to pursue this is pretty simple. When I look around, I do not see any women who are at the same status level as Tony Robbins. This is really disheartening, and although I may not achieve the same professional status as a Tony Robbins, I can certainly aspire to be the female version of him. Why not? What have I got to lose for trying to take this path? An even better question would be, what if I am successful in achieving the Tony Robbins status I am going after? How cool would that be?

So, what am I doing to get there? I can't reveal everything I am doing, but I can tell you I am going to pursue this in a way I've never done before. What can you do to help me? You can encourage and support me in my endeavors to achieve the professional status I seek.

By reading this, you are helping me develop my personal brand — a challenge with such a common name. (I have often thought I should start up a Kathleen Murphy club, as I would have hundreds, if not thousands, of women to enlist. Perhaps they could be some of my early adopters, although this could be quite confusing when I really stop to think about it.)

My point is that, given the current state of our country and how divided we are on so many points, including the pro-women movement, I believe this is the ideal time to come forward to serve as a strong role model. Women, especially, need to be motivated, given all of the challenges we routinely face in both business and life. Women also need to be inspired to keep going, despite the odds they may face to succeed. I never imagined the proverbial "glass ceiling" would still exist today.

I also did not think women would still have to contend with the type of treatment we are still dealing with as we move into the next decade. The reality is that harassment is still an issue, but I am hopeful all of the attention on this topic will spark conversations to begin the process of reducing this kind of conduct. Some day, it may not have to be tolerated in the workplace or in society.

Elsewhere in this book, you can read about what you can do to be inspired, or how you can aspire to be someone other than you may be now. I sincerely believe it is possible to do so; however, it will require the right amount of support and the will to achieve what may seem impossible.

I remember seeing the word *impossible* broken down into three words – *I am possible*. When you change your attitude and direct your energy towards either a single-minded mission or series of goals that are in strong alignment, look out! For me, this has always been the recipe to achieve anything I set my mind to.

It has taken me many years to get to this point, but I feel ready to have the next chapter in my life start unfolding. I know how I want it to be written, and exactly how it will play out. I have a vision for where I am going. I look forward to this amazing journey, one I hope you will be on with me, as it is going to be more fun and rewarding than just about anything I have ever done, and only short of having an amazing family and friend support system in place.

| Progress: Are You Making Some? |

Today was an exceptional day, one I have been waiting to experience for more years than you can imagine. What I saw today was progress. Not the kind of quick movement we all tend to favor, but the kind that takes multiple decades to achieve. It wasn't my progress, but someone I have known most of my life who has always inspired me.

Sometimes you can recognize progress. Usually, though, it takes much longer to see or experience any type of forward motion. There are many ways to measure progress. In the high-tech marketing world I worked in, just about every project was measured. This was normal to me, but not every job has this high level of what I refer to as "disciplined scrutiny."

Feeling like you are under the microscope every day can be exhausting, and more stressful than I care to think about. Although it can take its toll, especially if you don't know how to inject a sense of counter balance into the mix, being professionally trained to make progress on a daily basis does have benefits.

Let me tell you about a friend who was also a former client — I helped her to produce her first jazz CD. For most of our lives, she has been the complete opposite of me in almost everything we each did professionally. When I would give her marketing, branding, or business advice, she ignored my suggestions and did the the exact opposite.

As you can imagine for someone like me used to carefully measuring progress, working with her at times was incredibly frustrating, but I knew what we were working on would pay off one day. I just didn't know how long it would take. Fast forward almost 20 years. As we reconnected, she reminded me how I used to tell her, "I know the person who can accomplish her goals is hiding in you, and will some day make her debut."

Well this day arrived, and for the first time I witnessed an example of progress being made as I watched her giving a voice lesson to a promising future Broadway singer. Teaching voice lessons and getting paid to do so has always been something my friend wanted to do, and she was doing this right in front of me.

The next example of progress I saw from my friend occurred as she was listening to financial advice. I later learned that she took the next step and scheduled a time to review and put into action the financial advice given to her. She *was* listening to me after all!

This woman had always wanted to make a living from her ability to sing. After more than two and a half decades of pursuing this dream, it is now a reality. Her achievement took far longer than I imagined, but it did happen. The best part is that her progress is accelerating at an exponentially swift pace. She now has perspective on what it means to achieve the kind of progress she desired.

My friend has always believed in her ability to be able to make a living from her natural gift, but the most gratifying part is seeing her now realize long-held goals, including living in an artist's loft in New York City. The most remarkable part of where she lives today is that she only came across this space after she lost her last apartment and everything in it to a building fire. Luckily, she and her dog were out walking when the fire occurred, and no one was hurt.

How progress is measured depends on the type of work you are doing, and often can be subjective. My profession is a creative one, designed to have a positive influence on people. The measurements are unique to the work I do. My point is that even a small amount of progress can be beneficial.

Sometimes it is important to take time to celebrate our small wins, as over time they accumulate and can produce amazing results. My friend is a great illustration of this. I hope you will soon have your own examples of progress you can appreciate.

This page is dedicated to my long-time friend Ellen O'Brien, who also happens to be an incredibly talented jazz and Broadway singer. Listen to some of her songs at store.cdbaby.com/cd/ellenobrien.

| The Benefits of Travel |

The first time I flew on an airplane was a trip from Boston to Newark to visit my college roommate, Michelle Kessler-Sanders. I was 20 years old and both nervous and excited. As the plane took off, I looked out the window and realized this was something I intended to do more of — travel, that is. I recommend you do the same. Seeing the world is life changing.

Not having had the opportunity to travel outside of New England until I was 20 certainly formulated my initial world view. I knew there were many things I could learn from travel. So, when I began my career search, I looked for positions that would allow me to travel. That was one of the best decisions I ever made, as it changed my life.

I appreciate the fact not all jobs come with the chance to travel, but if there is the slightest opportunity, do not let it pass. Simply taking one trip will introduce you to a whole new world of possibilities. First, traveling offers the opportunity to see places far different from where you live. Although some of the differences are subtle, you will notice. Keep a list of your favorites: For example, in the U.S., soda vs. pop, hoagies vs. subs, packies vs. liquor stores . . . you get the idea.

No matter where you travel, you will have a chance to meet new people. My family will confirm that talking to people is one of my top five favorite things to do! Decades later, I am still in contact with folks I have met from all over the globe.

Traveling to other parts of the U.S., you will see that others live basically the same way you do, with some exceptions for extreme climates such as Alaska or Hawaii. Appreciating that others around the country have similar living challenges can be a uniting element, especially if you live in an area that is very homogeneous.

When you travel outside the U.S., you will have an opportunity to go through Customs and the border of the country to which you are traveling. No two experiences in doing this have ever been the same for me. Recently I had the good fortune of traveling to Fiji. Going through Customs, I noticed numerous signs forbidding carrying food into their country, which can potentially introduce harmful elements. I was traveling from Sydney, Australia, where I had purchased some mixed nuts. Luckily, I remembered they were in my suitcase and threw them out. Otherwise I would have been fined $400. The point is, pay attention to things you might not normally need to worry about when you are traveling locally.

Take photos of the places you visit. "A traveler without observation," said Persian poet Saadi, "is a bird without wings." You will appreciate looking back on these images for years to come, and photos are a way to share your experiences with others. Date them, and add the names and contact information of people you met. If there is a strong connection that could lead to business, be sure to follow up with a note when you return home.

When you start traveling internationally, you'll notice the different regional customs in each of the countries you visit. One company I worked for trained me to learn about the customs of the people in the places where I would be traveling. For example, in Japan, silence really *is* golden and valued over chatter. If you're traveling on business, making connections in a foreign country is critical. Observing another culture's etiquette opens doors to more successful communications.

We know that other countries may do basic things differently, whether it's their currency, driving rules, or living arrangements. Whenever I have a chance, I visit a local market to see how different items are displayed. I also look at the packaging, which is often unique. Seeing common things in a different way is part of what makes traveling fun.

Every time I travel, I am pleased with how genuinely nice people are. Getting away from home can open your mind to the fact that most people are decent human beings.

Seek out as many travel opportunities as you can, even if you have to pay for them yourself. Be prepared to see the world through an entirely new lens. A well-traveled person is fascinating, adopts an international circle of friends, and is able to tap into many more resources than one who stays put.

So, where is your next trip? Perhaps I'll see you there.

‖ Enjoy the Journey ‖

There is something to be said about making sure you take time to stop and smell the roses. Given the busy lives and professional careers we have, we often get caught up in focusing only on the destination. We forget about taking time to enjoy the journey as part of the process. With this, the 100th story I penned in 2018, I'm doing just that.

My paternal grandmother Catherine lived to celebrate 102 birthdays. When anyone would ask her what it was like to live to such a ripe old age, she would generally reply that her life had been an unbelievable journey. She also added something about how important it was to appreciate the time you have each day, the people who are in your life, and whatever type of good health you enjoy.

Up until about six weeks before she passed away, my grandmother was completely cognizant of her environment. She was also incredibly cheerful, aware of what was going on in the world, especially if the news had to do with the Boston Red Sox.

Just a few weeks prior to passing on, she demanded to be taken to get her nails and hair done, along with insisting, despite her doctor's wishes, that she enjoy a canned Starbucks cappuccino every day. Her theory was that she should be able to have at least one vice she could enjoy. I agree.

Sometimes, when we are so focused on completing our work, we lose sight of the importance of taking the time to relish what we are doing. If you are in a career that is project- or service-based, the work will likely still be there tomorrow if you do not complete it today.

Friends who are in the research field seem to be especially good at understanding the process of enjoying the journey. They recognize that it is the process itself that might lead to discovering new scientific evidence to help cure diseases. Knowing they are on a journey of discovery allows them to savor the time, energy, and commitment to work that can be so rewarding.

When I set out to write my first blog in 2018, I did not have a vision of writing 100. However, after finishing two dozen or so, I decided I should set a goal — complete 100 articles by the end of the year. As I wrote about topics that intrigued me, or subjects that people had asked me to share my insight on, I thought about how it would make sense to package them into a book.

The concept started taking shape and direction as I was about four months into the writing process. I noticed that most of the articles were on topics I wish I had insight to as an upcoming business executive when I was in my 20s, 30s and 40s. The inspiration to continue was to challenge myself each month to have a target of how many I needed to complete to reach my year-end goal.

In late October 2018, I had only completed 40 articles, so I set myself an ambitious goal of completing 30 in 15 days. These blogs were written when I was in both Australia and Fiji. Many of the topics were inspired by the people I met in my travels.

When I returned from my trip in mid-November, I still had another 30 to write. So, I once again set out on a mission to complete them before the end of December. You're now reading the fruits of that labor!

The part of this journey that continues to be the most rewarding, and that I look forward to next year and beyond, is to have a positive impact on readers. I sincerely hope each one will benefit in some small way from me sharing my knowledge about both life and business.

Update: I am on track to finish book Number 4! Book Number 3 will be published in late 2020, or early 2021.

| Focus On Joy |

Something that you may think is fleeting doesn't have to be. It is the feeling of joy. There are people who epitomize the essence of joy. One is my dear friend Anna Maria Soriano. This story is a tribute to her, and how the word "joyful" perfectly encapsulates who she was. Being joyful is how she lived each day. Everyone needs at least one person like Anna Maria in their lives, and my life and others won't be the same without her.

Do you have someone in your life who, when you are around them, you simply cannot think about anything negative? I hope you do, as I did. However, I lost this dear friend to her battle with cancer on December 18, 2017. Her name is Anna Maria Soriano.

We met each other while working at Constant Contact. She was on the sales team, I was on the marketing team. When I first met her, I had the feeling I had met her at some other point in my life. We became instant friends. She was also the type of colleague who you could count on, no matter what. She would always go well beyond delivering in any circumstance — what at Constant Contact we referred to as "Wow."

Anna Maria grew up in the North End of Boston. For those unfamiliar with the area, it is referred to as the Italian section in Boston.

Anna Maria took great pride in having grown up in the North End. She loved sharing stories of what it was like to grow up there, including the neighborhood debate about whether Mike's Pastry or Modern Pastry was the better bakery. Her favorite was Modern Pastry. Magically every time I visited her home, she had Modern Pastry treats on the table. Having a sweet tooth, this was a perfect arrangement for me, and if you have ever had a treat from Modern, you know how hard it is to say no to the offer of one of their confections.

While we worked together at Constant Contact, I learned a number of things from Anna Maria. One of them was that your voice and its tone could influence people. I also learned from her how people paid attention differently when you fully leveraged the power of your vocal cords.

And Anna Maria was literally the "voice" of Constant Contact. When you called into the company, it was her voice you heard to direct you to whom you were trying to reach. She also was the lead webinar producer of content for the last five years of her life. This included giving live presentations around the country.

Her voice was infectious. She captured your attention and made you want to pay attention to everything she was teaching you. Although you may have thought her voice and the way she presented her material was an act, it wasn't. It was genuinely who she was. The best part? After talking to her, you could not help but feel better or more enthused.

No one is immune from having a bad day. However, it was not possible to end your day on a negative note if you worked with Anna Maria, or had the fortune of being her friend. She made every day you worked with her fun and interesting. She also challenged you to see the joy in whatever it was you were working on.

Often when we chatted, Anna Maria talked about wanting to travel, specifically to Italy. This was one of the places on her bucket list. I was thrilled when she told me she was going to take a trip there the summer of 2017. With Stage 4 cancer, this meant she had to time her trip around her cancer treatments. If you saw any of the photos she took on her trip to Italy, you could see the joy on her face of being there.

Attitude plays a large role in whether you can find and have joy in your life. My dear friend Anna Maria was able to accomplish this every day. How? Because of her amazing attitude.

I wish more people could be like Anna Maria, and I hope to embrace her concept of incorporating joy into every aspect of my life. I hope you do, too.

Rest in peace my dear friend. Thank you for teaching me to be able to find the joy in all aspects of my life. I will never forget you, and your memory will live on in my heart and soul.

Chapter 3 | Work Tips

|| 9 Reasons Manners Will Get You Ahead in Business ||

Most people have been taught basic manners, but many have forgotten to apply them regularly. In both life and business scenarios, having and using manners can make a difference. Whether you realize it or not, you are being judged on your use of them.

At the core of our best behavior are the fundamental manners we learned as children. Granted, some people may have been exposed to more manners than others, but most adults learned the basics, which include saying thank you, excusing yourself if you bump into or interrupt someone, holding a door as a courtesy to others, and looking someone in the eye as you shake their hand. These are just a few of the foundational manners, and although they are still put to use every day, not everyone is applying them as often as they should.

One of the most common offenses is not saying *thank you* to someone who did something for you. It could be as simple as handing you a piece of paper, paying you a compliment, taking time to explain something, or pressing the elevator button for your floor. Acknowledging another person's act should always be a reason for thanking them. So, why do so many people you interact with in business or outside of work seem to have hit *pause* on their manners?

Not applying your manners can actually work against you. Indeed, even if you are a good person and kind to others, if you do not apply your manners regularly, you will be considered less often for future opportunities, potentially putting career advancement in jeopardy. I know this from years of working with, mentoring, and witnessing those who did not apply their manners in each situation. I've seen the negative outcomes. Here are eight ways using your manners can propel your future career:

1| People who consistently use good manners are considered to be more thoughtful and aware of others.

2| Using your manners regularly gives the perception that you have learned how to appropriately conduct yourself appropriately in numerous scenarios. This could lead to others including you in opportunities you might otherwise miss.

3| Those who apply their manners are perceived as being more emotionally intelligent.

4| More people want to interact with those who have manners, as they appear to be more even-tempered and pleasant to be around.

5| Even if you were not born with the proverbial silver spoon in your mouth, as long as you exercise basic manners, people will give you more of a chance to interact with them, right from the start.

6| People with manners tend to get introduced to more people. Making new connections will indirectly provide you with additional opportunities.

7| A hand-written thank-you note, especially in the age of digital communication, really stands out, and is appreciated by the recipient. Writing a thank-you note also demonstrates your ability to communicate well, and expresses a sincere appreciation of the other person's time or an act of kindness.

8| I have spoken to hundreds of people who have expressed a dislike of someone because they were rude or didn't say *thank you*. But they would never tell the person they dislike them because of their lack of manners. Just imagine how many more people might get along if they simply utilized their manners?

If you grew up in a family that did not teach you manners, or you missed any manner-related lessons being taught in school, there is still time to learn the fundamentals, and start applying them. It's worth the effort!

| 8 Tips to Keep Your Creative Juices Flowing |

Everyone possesses a bit of creativity. It's true! Some people either do not have the opportunity to discover their abilities, or dismiss this talent as unimportant. Being a creative person, and having used this skill in business from Day One, it is hard to imagine not accessing this talent.

Just about everyone has held a Crayon™, and also likely created something with it. You may not recall your first drawing, or when you did it, but the experience may have been the catalyst to ignite your creativity.

When we are growing up, any number of experiences we had could have had a positive impact on whether or not we wanted to incorporate creativity into our personal or professional lives. Thinking back on your early creative experiences, do you remember one of them having an impact?

Regardless of the role you play in business, there is always a way to incorporate creative thinking into what you are doing — and to enhance it, too. One of the ways is through brainstorming.

Essentially, brainstorming is a creative way to problem solve or come up with innovative ideas. Brainstorming can be done individually, but it is far more effective when multiple people are involved.

If you are new to brainstorming, begin thinking of a challenge you are trying to solve, then write the challenge on paper, a whiteboard, or your laptop. For some reason, I have found working with paper and whiteboards an easier way to visualize possible solutions. Seeing the words will help you recognize other connections. Add these new word links, and continue the process.

After working on this word association for 10-20 minutes, you will eventually see a pattern of potential solutions emerge. If you do not, and are working alone, bring one or two others into your brainstorming session. Choose people who you deem to be good problem solvers, strong communicators, analytical thinkers, or creative idea people. There isn't a perfect combination of people to help you to brainstorm, so do not worry about who can help, as most people will have something to contribute.

Here are eight ways to access and optimize your creativity:

1| Take a five-minute break from what you are working on, especially if you feel tired or uninspired, and do just about anything else, like take a quick walk, get a drink of water, or chat with a colleague.

2| Tune out, literally, and listen to your favorite songs to clear your mind.

3| Take out a piece of paper and begin doodling, creating random objects or non-sensical designs.

4| Look online at photos of nature, or images that inspire you (and that are sanctioned by HR, of course).

5| Make a quick phone call to say hello to someone you have not spoken to recently. Tell them you only have two to three minutes to talk, and stick to this time frame.

6| Take a walk in a nearby park, visit a museum, or go to a high school play. Most school performances are quite affordable, and the quality of the production may be much better than you expect.

7| Keep some Silly Putty™ or Play Doh™ in your desk drawer. Take five minutes to create something, anything — snowballs, logs, smiley faces. Just use your imagination or look around you and mimic something you see. If you can find a mini version of Jenga™ or Legos,™ keep it handy to also tap into your creative building skills.

8| Re-arrange things on your desk, or in a small area that will take less than 10 minutes to complete. The new arrangement will help alter your perspective, and get your creative juices flowing again.

Although some people who claim they are not creative might tackle challenges purely from an analytical perspective, they can still find room to factor creative thinking into their approach if they can remain open-minded. So, the next time you are feeling less creative, give some of these suggestions a try.

| 10 Ways to Know It's Time to Leave Your Company |

Far too many people remain in a job well past the point of when they should have moved on. Too many people become complacent or comfortable with where they are, and others fear the unknown. There is nothing wrong with being afraid, but risk adversity is what tends to keep people in their current roles or at a company beyond when they should be there. Is it time for you to make a move, and how do you know?

Gone are the days of gold watches to honor 25 years of service. Working in the computer technology space the majority of my career has likely influenced my thinking about why it is important to not linger too long at a company. What is too long? This will vary based on the industry, the role, the company — whether it's a start-up or a well-established business, for example, and countless other factors. It is not always a straightforward decision; however, there are signs to help you decide.

Has anyone ever told you it might be time to move on from your current job? If you are like others, you either dismissed the suggestion, or you refused to consider there may be some truth in what they were saying. If you are new to the work force, you may not have heard anyone telling you, "It's time;" but fair warning – you probably will at some point.

Sometimes the people who make the suggestion have ulterior motives, but most simply have your best interests in mind. Pay attention to who is telling you that maybe it's time to move on. Have they had the experience of going through this before, maybe more than once?

Working in the technology field has influenced my thinking on why people should only remain at a company for about four or five years. Why? Because in this field, the best way to learn and grow professionally is to gain the experience one can only obtain by moving around.

Working at a new company allows you to experience different management styles and cultures. You will also be exposed to new systems, processes, and technologies that can positively influence the way you perform your job. Review these other reasons to leave your company, plus other factors to consider when deciding if it's time to move on:

1| You feel like you are in a rut and are not being challenged, even when you ask to be considered for new projects.

2| Your level of responsibility has either stayed the same or decreased.

3| You have been passed over for numerous potential promotions.

4| Your gut tells you that your manager no longer supports your career growth.

5| Others you work with have stopped including you in on communications, when in the past they routinely would have.

6| Sunday evening you start to dread the thought of going into work the next day.

7| Your internal work network has stagnated, and you now only find satisfaction from engaging with others outside your company.

8| The work you are doing has become too routine. You find it hard to focus because you are bored.

9| You are more excited about hearing what your peers at other companies are doing, versus the work you are tackling.

10| Any joy you once experienced is but a pleasant memory. You have tried to recreate this feeling, but all attempts seem futile.

Life is short — eat dessert first! This quirky expression can apply to your work situation as well as dinner. Because you spend so much of your quality time at the office, you should enjoy what you are doing. Knowing when to leave can seem — is — difficult. Most people do not press ahead until they have been suffering in their role or at their company past the point of when they should have made a decision.

If you don't think you are ready to begin exploring other options, take another look at the points above and consider your responses. Now, go out and start the exploration process for your next job. I guarantee you will enjoy the experience.

|| 7 Ways to Know What to Say Next ||

You made it past the polite introduction, but what do you say next? Some folks have mastered the art of small talk, or even more advanced conversation, while others continue to struggle with their communication abilities. What if you could easily and fluidly move to the next topic?

So, you just met the person you have admired, are about to work for, or want to get to know on a deeper level. But you are perplexed about how to take the conversation past an introductory phase. Perhaps you can carry on a dialogue for a few minutes, but it feels like agony. You begin to feel your nerves shake and start to stumble over words. You are not alone. There is hope for you to intuitively know what to say next.

Why is it that some people are born with the gift of gab? Some of it comes naturally, but the rest has to do with practice. So, what's the secret to having a comfortable conversation?

The first thing you have to do is be willing. Don't let fear get the best of your intentions to become a stronger, more fluid communicator. The next step is to find someone with whom to practice and commit to regular sessions.

Unlike common sense, having the gift of being able to converse easily with others can be developed. There is presently no school for common sense — you either have it or you don't. Here are some tips you can use to improve your communication abilities:

1| Make sure you are listening to what is being said. Some people get caught up thinking about how to respond. They make the mistake of not fully paying attention to what the person they are talking to is actually saying.

2| While you are paying attention to what is being said, be mindful of the person's body language. Maintaining eye contact and body awareness are foundational to smooth communication.

3| When you start a conversation, make sure your body posture is strong, you are facing them directly, and your voice is at a level they can hear.

4| As you listen to what the person is saying, think about a question or a response you would want someone to ask you. If you are not sure what to say next, ask the person if they could go into further detail about what they said. This will give you more time to think about what to ask them next, and will extend the conversation.

5| If you are at a complete loss for what to say, ask their opinion on a topic that is general enough, but related to the environment you are in at the moment. It's best not to delve into politics or religion, at least at first!

6| Check the news now and then to see what topics are trending. You are bound to have an opinion, and so will the person or people with whom you will be speaking. You can leverage your knowledge of what is in the news to extend your chat, and from there, take the conversation in many different directions.

7| Think like a reporter, who asks questions to extract the information they need to write their articles. Just remember *Who, What, When, Where, Why, and How.* Having this arsenal of leading words can work like magic.

Now that you have a few techniques and tips on how to extend a conversation, go out and practice. At some point, you will realize you are beginning to master the art of conversation. This new skill will open up a whole new world of possibilities, and you will have many new people with which to converse. This is going to be fun!

| 10 Things You Should Never Say Via Email |

Do you know the unwritten rules of what not to say in an email? Verbally putting your foot in your mouth is one thing. But emailing some kinds of information can put you in a difficult situation — one you should avoid.

In some cases, having a paper trail or an email to substantiate claims can be beneficial in business. But there are unwritten rules about recording certain content via elecronic mail that might be taken the wrong way, or worse, end up as cause for your dismissal.

Not everyone is born with common sense, the kind that helps keep you from making a *faux pas*. Even if you were graced with common sense, you still may not have a complete understanding of the unwritten taboos of sharing information electronically.

There are plenty of topics that are perfectly acceptable to communicate in writing, but it is more important to understand which ones to avoid, especially if you want to keep your job. If you are new to the business world, someone who does not regularly communicate via email, or simply want to avoid sticky situations, keep reading.

Here are 10 subjects that are not acceptable to share and communicate via email:

1| Never criticize the recipient's response when you reply to their email. Avoid words or phrases that could be perceived as a personal attack.

2| Do not state any private opinions you have about this person, or others, in an email. Some examples include references to religion, politics, sexual orientation, and ethnic background.

3| Do not state in writing how you feel about the email you received. For example, don't say it has upset or angered you. Craft responses that are neutral in tone.

4| If you think what you are saying could, at some point, be either embarrassing or even slightly inappropriate, then it likely is. Re-write your message.

5| Ensure that your content is professional. Keep business and personal communications separate.

6| Unless you manage the person and are having a discussion either with Human Resources or your boss, discussing other people you work with and their performance is not acceptable, even if it is complimentary.

7| Do not make inferences or speculate about your company or the people with whom you work. The comments may be misread.

8| Sharing or telling jokes in an email can get you into trouble. What you think is funny and inoffensive could be the opposite for the recipient(s). Don't take that chance.

9| Making unsolicited suggestions to the recipient is not recommended. However, if you ask them, in writing, if they would like ideas or feedback, then you are in a safer place since you have their permission.

10| Don't tell the person with whom you are communicating that you plan to quit your job. This information could be sent to your boss, and you might not like the outcome, unless you actually intend to turn in your resignation that day.

| 5 Ways to Deal With High Maintenance Colleagues |

Why is it that people who are what is referred to as high maintenance so unaware that they are this way? And if they are aware they are, they often tell you that's just who they are, and you will have to deal with them that way. Whether they realize they are or not, high maintenance people are challenging — and exhausting — to work with. Here are some ways to deal with high maintenance colleagues.

No one wants to be labeled as high maintenance. A "high maintenance" person is similar to passive aggressive individuals, as they can be unpleasant to be around. Nothing ever seems to be done right, fast enough, slow enough, or even close to how they think it should be done. They are demanding and often hypercritical of everything.

Every. Little. Detail.

One of the most frustrating aspects of high maintenance people is that they think they have communicated why you should have already done what they are complaining about, when it's obvious that they often are not strong at articulating what they expected to be done, or how to tackle or complete the task. When you are being criticized by a high maintenance person, it generally is due to their lack of satisfaction based on their inability to properly express themselves.

Even if someone knows they are high maintenance and tells you they are, it doesn't make dealing with them any easier. Do we need to deal with their exhausting demands and uptight personality all the time? Yes, and no. Yes, we have to interact with them; but no, we do not have to allow their stress-inducing personality to ruin our day.

The better question to ask is how did they become this way, and do they enjoy it?

When you have to work with someone who is considered to be in the high maintenance category, there are things you can do to help them to become more tolerable. It will take patience on your part, but for your own sanity, it will be worth the effort. Here are a few tips you can apply to make working with a high maintenance colleague more tolerable:

1| Since poor communication is at the heart of a high maintenance attitude, you will have to help them with becoming better at expressing their expectations, either in writing or verbally. When the person starts to verbally express their displeasure about what you are working on, ask them to explain how they would do it differently, and whether they would be satisfied if it were done their way.

2| One of the ways I deal with difficult people, especially when they are being verbally abusive, is to ask them a simple question: "Why did you say that?" Continue to ask this same question until you are satisfied with their explanation, or until you receive an apology, if one is warranted. Asking for an explanation will disarm the verbal abuser and put him or her in a position to really think about what they said.

3| Tell your disgruntled colleague you are going to step away and will be happy to resume the conversation when they are ready to start acting and speaking in a more reasonable manner.

4| There is a concept of strength in numbers. If the high maintenance person is being more difficult in a one-on-one scenario, stop the interaction, and only resume when you have the support of one or two other people to help deflect their negative attitude. Leverage the support of others to tone down, or abate the high maintenance act you are having to deal with individually.

5| When you are at a point in the interaction when you can tell they are really frustrated, ask why they are feeling this way. Asking them to explain their emotional attitude will get them to express why they are acting the way they are, and give them time to diffuse their frustration by having you call them out on their actions.

We cannot change people, they can only change themselves if they want to. But having coping mechanisms can lessen your burden. Sometimes by pointing out undesirable behavior can, over time, get them to become more introspective, and potentially, less high maintenance.

|| 5 Ways to Recognize Career Burnout ||

Let's face facts: It's difficult to avoid stress, but that doesn't mean there aren't things you could be doing to lessen or avoid stressors. What are you doing to protect yourself from occupational burnout?

Not having stress in your life is certainly an idealistic concept, yet one that is elusive to most professionals. Studies reveal that some level of stress can be helpful. But how do you really measure that? Perhaps by taking your blood pressure, or by the frequency you get headaches at work.

Oddly, burnout can sometimes sneak up on you, although it typically has been building momentum long before you recognize the symptoms. Learn to recognize the signs:

1| You have lost enthusiasm for doing the work you at one time could not wait to start doing each day.

2| Every day you seem to have less energy to invest in giving the 100% effort you easily used to put to your work.

3| You are more irritated with yourself or your colleagues about trivial matters that in the past would have never given you pause.

4| Looking forward to taking on more responsibility or advancing in your profession does not interest or inspire you like it once did.

5| When you are on vacation, or taking short breaks from your work over the weekend, you dread the thought of returning.

Stress and burnout are difficult. Do not ignore the warning signs. The consequences of doing so can bring upon health risks, such as depression and high blood pressure.

Fortunately, there are a number of ways to help eliminate stress. A few good friends have become yoga instructors, and they changed professions to do so. One had earned an MBA and was a high-level financial analyst; another, a Registered Nurse; and the third self-employed. All three made the decision to switch professions due to their job stress, and because they wanted to live healthier lives, and teach others how to do so, too.

Yoga is one stress-reduction method. Other forms of relaxing exercise include stretching, Tai Chi, and Qigong. Another kind of stress relief is meditation, which can be practiced just about anywhere, anytime, and for relatively short periods. It's possible to feel the positive impact from meditation in as little as five to ten minutes. Both yoga and meditation help change the way you breathe to increase the stress-relieving effects of these practices. I do not proclaim to be either a yoga or meditation expert by any stretch of the imagination, but I have taken enough classes and have had enough instruction to legitimately claim they both work well. If you are lucky enough to work for a company that offers employees these kinds of stress-reducing benefits (e.g., on-site massage, aromatherapy, or nap or meditation areas) consider taking full advantage.

Another way to reduce your stress level is to evaluate your daily diet. Consuming more nutritional foods can increase energy and cognitive abilities, and make you feel much better mentally and physically. Contact a nutritionist or healthy friend who can help you to review your current diet and create a plan to become a healthier consumer. Check your company's health plan. You may have benefits that provide you with funds to apply towards a gym membership or nutritionist.

Although most insurance companies have not fully embraced the concept of acupuncture, if you have one that does, investigate the benefits associated with this eastern medicine practice.

Doing simple, free activities such as taking a walk in nature, or listening to relaxing music could also contribute to stress reduction. Pandora and other popular on-line radios offer relaxation-focused music, or "spa stations." I've found them to be even more relaxing than some classical stations, which normally are very therapeutic.

Please take time to address your physical and mental health, as you will need to have both of these in good working form so you can enjoy your life more when you are not as focused on your career.

‖ 5 Ways to Manage Your Boss ‖

I hear it all the time — you know, the age-old story about how your boss is driving you crazy. It doesn't have to be this way! It is quite possible you are simply not managing him or her well. Here are five ways you can secretly, and effectively, manage your boss.

Unless you are your own boss, you have probably uttered the words, or thought to yourself at one point or another, "My boss is driving me crazy!"

Based on the dynamics of the typical boss and subordinate roles, it is likely that you will be annoyed by your boss now and then. This is normal, especially when the work is mainly assigned to you, without the ability to decline or limit the amount of tasks coming your way. Or is there?

Perhaps you have heard that everything is negotiable? It really is, but not everyone feels comfortable negotiating, so they simply accept the work that flows their way. Those who have developed negotiating skills, even minor ones, tend to be much more satisfied with their bosses. Why? Because they are indirectly *managing* their boss. The best part of having a negotiating conversation with your boss, is that they may not be aware of the fact they are being managed by you!

So, if you are thinking, "I do not like to negotiate, and my communication or debating skills are not up to the task," keep reading. If you can talk, you have to ability to develop your negotiation skills.

At its basic level, negotiating is about asking questions. You can do that! By asking questions about the assignment, your boss will be forced to confront whether what he or she is asking has been fully thought through. You might be surprised how many times they have not thoroughly considered what they are asking you to do, and are only serving as a middle man pushing assignments down from above.

Negotiating also allows you to obtain clarity on aspects of work, such as timeframe flexibility, who else can or should be involved in the work, and how the project outcome will be benchmarked and measured.

Here are five recommendations on how to manage your boss:

1| On Monday, assess the mood of your boss by having a brief conversation, or by checking in with one of your colleagues. If they are in a less than favorable mood, leave them alone until mid-day and then reassess. Monday mornings can be stressful. The beginning of the week is a popular time for upper management team meetings to review the status of the business. Even if the stats are on track, this can impact your supervisor's mood.

2| Make sure you have a weekly assigned time to check in with your boss, even if it is for only 10 minutes. During your meetings with your boss, make sure you are driving the meeting, and have set the agenda. Setting the agenda puts you in charge. In essence, you are managing your boss.

3| Clarify monthly or quarterly expectations for your goals — critical to managing your boss. As long as you are clear about the project and results of your work, and confirming during your weekly meetings that priorities have not changed, you will be in strong alignment with their expectations.

4| Get to know your boss. Take time to go out to lunch or coffee with him or her once or twice a month to have a non-work conversation. If you do not do this, you run the risk of them not seeing you as a whole person, with a unique personality they may not be able to observe in the office. I understand people work remotely and may not have many opportunities to meet with their boss in person, but when you do, make sure you go through this same exercise.

5| Ask your boss to articulate how you can help them with professional network connections to make them look good. This may seem awkward, but ask anyway, as most people do not know the answer, and may be entirely wrong by making incorrect assumptions.

Depending on your career level, some of these suggestions will need to be modified, but they have been applied successfully by people who are just starting out, all the way to the highest c-suite executives.

‖ 5 Ways to Get Along With Others ‖

Kindergarten is one of the most important years of our lives, as it sets the foundation for learning how to interact with others — arguably one of the most underrated skills we acquire in our formative years.

Like most people, you probably did not realize just how important that first year of school was ... and why would you — you were a five-year-old with limited life skills. But, as Robert Fulghum, author of *All I Really Need to Know I Learned in Kindergarten*, proclaims, we really *were* all taught some critical life skills — like how to get along.

Have you heard of the expression, "Play nice in the sandbox?" This is one of the fundamental elements associated with getting along with others, and consists of being polite and respectful of others. Savvy executives know that if they don't follow the simple lessons they learned in Kindergarten, they risk getting thrown out of the sandbox.

Have you ever considered how you actually met people, and maintained those friendships and relationships? Chances are you learned these skills a long time ago from your parents and primary school teachers, yet you were blissfully unaware of the fact you were developing these abilities. Sometimes I wonder if some people skipped Kindergarten, were napping through the "how to get along with others" lessons, or were too distracted with anything else to pay attention.

Most humans have a pretty well-developed fraud meter, and can easily tell when someone is not being sincere. We have all encountered people like this. It is uncomfortable to be around them, but I also feel sad for them. Why? Because they are unaware of how they are perceived, and likely wonder why they do not have many genuine friends.

There are fundamental elements associated with how to get along with others, but sometimes people either forget them, or, perhaps they did not learn them well. If you have ever wondered why some people seem to be gifted with being able to get along with others, I will let you in on a little secret: It is really not that hard to do. But you *will* have to make a genuine effort.

1| When you meet someone, ask how they are doing, and pay close attention to their answer. Most people will be polite and give you a brief response; use this as a starting point to advance the conversation.

2| Given the chance, ask the person where they grew up, and what led them to where they are today, either professionally or personally. People love to talk about themselves, so leverage this opportunity.

3| Ask the person if you can help them in some way, especially if you are their colleague. They may not take you up on your offer, but if you start a discussion about their current challenge, you can seize the opportunity to offer assistance. When you help a colleague, even if it is something as simple as making an introduction, they are more appreciative of this than you might imagine. Why? Because this is an example of being genuine, and you come across as being sincere.

4| Do something nice for the person you have met, the people you work with, or others you are getting to know. It doesn't have to be extravagant; it could simply be sharing an article or YouTube video related to the work you are doing. Do this over the course of a few weeks. (Just don't overdo it and be thought a stalker!) There are plenty of examples of nice gestures. The point is to be creative and do something for others that demonstrates how you are a genuinely nice person. This makes you more approachable and likeable.

5| Consider meeting people an opportunity to see the "diamond" beneath the surface. Don't get caught up thinking you need to be best friends with everyone. You do not; but at the same time, look at every encounter as a chance to uncover another layer of your new friend's personality. You will find that most people are interesting, gifted in their own way, and have a great deal to offer.

The bottom line is that you simply need to invest time in learning how to get along with others. Doing this is one of the most important skills to have in order to increase your future career options, and have access to an incredible network of fascinating people.

‖ 5 Ways to Stop Saying 'I'm Sorry' ‖

Being polite is a positive asset in most any situation. But there is one phrase that is overused, often when it's not even required: "I'm sorry." I have tried to weed this phrase from my garden of responses unless the situation truly warrants it. Why do we overuse this word, and why do we need to cut back?

I'm a big fan of showing and appropriately conveying respect in communications, but there is one word that I have noticed is overused. The word is *sorry*, typically expressed as *I'm sorry*.

Yes, it is appropriate to express genuine regret in numerous scenarios, but definitely not as often as this expression is uttered on a daily basis. One of the main reasons we over-use the expression is because it is a conditioned response, something we say when we do not know how to respond properly. When we utter apologies in instances when they are not required, it feels less genuine and can even come across as contrived.

More women than men apologize for instances when it is not required. Although it may seem trivial, reducing your use of this word will make expressing it when it is actually required much more impactful. Other people's perception of you can change when you stop apologizing for things that were not your fault or, on occasion, even your business. It simply makes sense to provide your words and expressions with sincerity for the greatest impact.

So how do you stop a habit you might not be aware of? One way is to pay more attention and be aware of how you express yourself.

This may sound ridiculous, but some people talk so much, they can barely recall what they have recently said. If you are a verbal faucet, being aware of this is the first step towards turning the tap down, or off, more often. Of course, I am not saying you need to cease communications with others. Just be more aware of how much you are talking.

Simply because you want to express yourself to others, whether they are your colleagues or friends, does not mean they want to hear what you have to say 24/7. There are times when it is appropriate not to say anything, or to be highly selective of your words. You have heard the expression, "Less is more." This can apply to conversations, too.

If you think you are an offender of over-using the words *I'm sorry*, review these tips to work towards only using them when it is actually appropriate.

1| Pay attention to what you are saying. See if you can catch yourself apologizing when it is not necessary.

2| Ask one of your trusted colleagues if they will honestly tell you if you over use the words *I'm sorry*.

3| When you are about to say *I'm sorry* when it is not appropriate or required, see if you can remain silent. This is similar to breaking the habit of saying *ummm* instead of pausing to think of the next word to say.

4| Create a few substitute expressions.

5| Commit to recognizing your over use of the phrase and challenge yourself to only express this sentiment when it is actually appropriate. After practicing this for one month, ask a few trusted colleagues if they have noticed you have reduced unnecessary apologies.

The greatest benefit you will gain from applying the words *I'm sorry* to your conversations appropriately? You and others will recognize that your words are far more genuine. The second benefit? You will come across to others as having a greater command of how you sincerely express empathy.

|| 5 Ways to Say 'No' ||

Why is a certain two-letter word such a difficult thing for people to say?
In some cultures, it is actually impolite to say "no," so they simply say
"yes," even when they actually mean "no." Many instances in both
business and in life require a resolute "no."

Words are a funny thing — even the really small ones can create a stunning impact depending upon how and when they are used.

Take, for example, the word *no*. This two-letter powerhouse can have enormous consequences, both positively and negatively.

When I worked at the Japanese company Hitachi, I quickly learned that the word *no* was not included in their lexicon. Culturally, Japanese do not use this word because they feel it is disrespectful. So, instead, they will tell you *yes*, when they really mean *no* — confusing communications. But with enough insight and practice, you can become adept at figuring out when *yes* actually means *no*.

At Hitachi, one of the ways I was able to ascertain when *yes* meant *no* was by asking questions. By asking enough of them, I was able to guide the conversation in a direction that allowed the Japanese colleague with whom I was chatting to comfortably let me know their response was *no* without actually saying so. Although a frustrating and lengthy process, in the end, it was worth the effort as it allowed us both to have a clear understanding of each other's points of view.

Conversely, in North America we, too, often have reservations about saying *no* when we mean *no*. In many business situations, we feel compelled to say *yes*, even when we know uttering this word is not going to guarantee successful results for either party involved. So, why do we place ourselves in this quandary? Why do we go to "get along?" Often it is because we do not want to disappoint others.

Think about politicians for a moment. When do you ever hear them say *no* (or *yes*, for that matter)? Instead, they dance around the issue, and divert to a topic that better serves their interests. This drives me crazy, which is probably why I can never imagine myself in politics!

Responding with *no* when we mean *no* can be easier if we remind ourselves to, "Say what you mean; mean what you say; but don't be mean when you say it."

And it takes practice. Try this Q&A to help you just say *no*!

1| Is the work time sensitive? If the response is *no*, ask if the task can wait to be done after your list of priorities is completed.

2| Where does the task fall on your priority list? If it is not even on the list, describe your list of priorities and ask (even if it's your boss) which one will need to be removed to accommodate the new request.

3| Ask what will happen if you cannot complete this task, or at least not until "x" period of time. You may be pleasantly surprised by the response (and the requestor will be impressed with your organization, assertiveness, and confidence).

4| Could a colleague take on the task? Staff may or may not be available, and indeed, the task might be something you should be doing, but, again, focus on prioritization of the task. If it does not have to be completed immediately, then you can say, "No, I cannot take on this project right now."

5| Dig deeper: Has the task been fully thought through? I have often found that requests to take on additional work have not always been thoroughly discussed to warrant spending precious time on them. To combat these random requests, ask if the project is in alignment with the corporate/company strategy, has a budget line item associated with it, or is a revenue-generating project. If the answer is *no* to each of these questions, then it will be easy for you to decline.

Naturally, you do not want to develop a reputation for being Captain No, but there are more instances when it is appropriate for you to say *no* than you think. When you say *no* you also secure time in your schedule to say *yes* to your priorities.

| 7 Tips to Help You Finish Strong |

I don't know exactly why, when you get close to finishing something, it seems like you might not get there. Or, why it feels harder to complete what you are doing when you are getting close to the finish line, regardless of what you are working on. But I've developed some techniques to help get over the finish line and finish strong.

It's the end of the month, quarter, or still yet, the end of the year, and the pressure you are under to hit your goals or your number is enormous. You might categorize your emotions as a love/hate relationship with your job right now.

Is it the adrenaline that keeps you coming back for more of the roller-coaster ride you seem to always be on? Or, perhaps as one sales person I know says, you are "coin operated" and driven to finish strong due to the monetary incentive for doing so.

If you ask most people who have deadline-driven careers, many of them will tell you they cannot imagine being in any other type of work scenario. Indeed, the first time most people experience the proverbial thrill of the chase to finish strong, they get hooked, so to speak. In my opinion, it is probably a good thing those who are under such pressure have at least a positive result to look forward to.

Yes, stress can be associated with producing positive results, such as during the last few days of the month when the sales team is chipping away at hitting their individual and team goals. A large part of achieving their goals has to do with believing they can do so themselves, and together with their teammates. All it takes is one person on the team who does not subscribe to this philosophy, and you know what happens? The dreaded self-fulfilling prophecy of not hitting the number. So how do you get everyone on board with being able to "finish strong?"

1| There is a saying, "Your team is only as strong as its weakest link." Identify the weakest link, and help them become stronger. It is typically up to the manager to do this, but sometimes colleagues have a better chance of making this happen.

2| Visualize the process of hitting your number. Challenge yourself and your team with personal daily goals that need to be met, or ideally, exceeded.

3| Put your goals literally in writing (not via a keyboard), and hang them up in front of where you sit. There is a powerful phenomenon that occurs when you manually record tasks on paper — you are more committed to making them happen.

4| Psyche yourself up! Talk to yourself and your team members, encouraging them to achieve their goals, and help contribute to the team goal.

5| Each time a negative thought about not hitting your goal creeps into your mind, dismiss the thought as irrational and untrue. Keep doing this anytime this happens until you stop thinking negatively.

6| Gain support from your marketing colleagues or others in the organization who are closely invested to cheering you and your team on to hit and exceed your numbers. Be creative with this approach, and ask them to genuinely participate in doing this.

7| Most importantly, believe in yourself, and know that you and your team members can and will hit the number.

Now that you have some tips to help you finish strong, go make it happen, as you have the power to do so. I believe in you!

This article is dedicated to Julius Johnson and the Channel Sales teams at Barracuda Networks.

‖ Do's and Don'ts of Holiday Parties ‖

Corporate holiday parties can seem like an innocent enough event. But, they are actually one of the annual rituals that can either help or hinder your professional standing. Even if you have attended a few holiday parties, each year there are numerous opportunities to potentially do something that can harm your career.

The holiday party landmines you step on can negatively impact your carefully-crafted reputation, and may also impact your career trajectory. Don't let mistakes you made at the holiday party have a negative effect on your job. Indeed, knowing the rules means you will be aware of the traps that can often get people into trouble. This will allow you to have a great time at the event because you know the rules of engagement. Don't be the person who treads into dangerous party territories that will make it a night of regrets, instead of a fun evening out with colleagues.

Don'ts:

Don't show up late to the party unless you have a really good reason.

Don't show up at the party already intoxicated or on some mind-altering drug. Liquid and other chemically-induced confidence, especially at a holiday party, can impact your normal, good decision-making process.

Don't over indulge in too much free booze, or load your plate with an absurd amount of food at the buffet. Neither of these will make you look good, and yes, people will notice.

Don't look like you are heading out to the local strip club to pick up your dancing shift at the end of the party. This applies to both men and women.

Don't dance as if you are trying to win a contest. This isn't the place to show off all your moves and call too much attention to yourself, even if you are professionally trained. Keep it low key.

Don't flirt with your co-workers' dates or your colleagues. If you haven't noticed, this has been a hot topic in the news lately.

Don't ask your boss or your boss' boss work-related questions. They are at the party to have a good time, too, and do not want to be talking shop.

Don't use your electronic gadgets. The point of this event is to engage with actual people. In person. Give your social media accounts a break, and enjoy actual face-to-face encounters with your colleagues and their guests. One exception is to take photos or videos at the event, but make sure they are not incriminating and you have permission to share or post them online.

Don't critique the event. The planning committee spent countless hours putting this event together for you to have a good time, and they volunteered their time to do so.

Do's:

Do consider volunteering to be on the event planning committee. Not only will it give you some visability at the event, it will put you in good standing with HR or the corporate team responsible for hosting the event.

Do think carefully about what perception people will have of the outfit you decided to wear, and err on being slightly more conservative.

Do arrive close to on-time. Being fashionably late at these kind of events is considered rude.

Do channel your best version of how you would act if you were being judged by the Charm School Committee.

Do consider sitting with at least one or two of your colleagues. Take time to talk to everyone on your team. Make sure you also talk to your boss, and introduce yourself to their date if they brought one.

Do participate in some of the planned activities available. Do try to have a good time, even if you have to fake it.

Do thank the people on the planning committee for putting on a great event, even if you did not have a good time. Send a thank-you email to the event planning committee when you return to work — they will appreciate the effort. An even better idea would be to write a quick, hand-written thank you note to the head of the planning committee.

Chapter 4 | Life Tips

‖ 6 Ways to Unplug and Recharge ‖

Too many people get caught in the trap of not taking time to recharge. Some employees are afraid to take time off, concerned that they will either miss out on big news, or be penalized. This kind of thinking is both paralyzing and short-sighted. Allocating down time is critical to both productivity and your well-being.

The United States has earned a reputation for "living to work" versus other countries who embrace the concept of "working to live." People in other countries have figured out the balance the need to infuse down time into their schedule. Granted, there are factors that make it more challenging to adopt this mindframe, but we can still increase the quality of our lives by taking more breaks, whether they are mental, physical, or both.

It never ceases to amaze me when people boast that they never take breaks or vacations and work all the time. What further astounds me is that they think that is a badge of honor. They are actually fooling themselves into thinking they are always highly productive. It is impossible to be at peak performance all of the time, especially when you do not take any breaks.

Humans need to take breaks. Studies show that after recharging, we all perform far better and are more creative and productive. Furthermore, studies show that even when people have accumulated the typical two-three weeks vacation time, most of them do not either use it, or are concerned about actually taking a vacation.

Do you avoid taking the down time that you and your body need? Learn how to stop, take a breath, and start embracing the benefits of down time.

1| Every few hours, get up and walk around, whether it's a stroll outside or just around your office. Changing your environment even for a short period of time can help you recharge, particularly when the sun is out and you get to experience it in person and not by viewing it from your office window.

2| Take a coffee or lunch break. At first, you might be tempted to incorporate some of your work into this time, but slowly ease yourself out of this practice.

3| If you are near a retail area, go window shopping — a visual vacation from what you are thinking about or looking at most of the day. You'll be pleasantly surprised how refreshed you'll feel when you get back to the task at hand. And who knows who you'll meet!

4| Plan a vacation or staycation. Having something to look forward to is a great way to be more inspired about your work. After you take the actual break, you will feel like a new person again. Sometimes just three days of doing something other than work, or better yet, fully relaxing, can put you in a much better frame of mind. Be amazed at the increased productivity when you return, refreshed and raring to go again.

5| Pick up a new hobby or volunteer your time and skills in an area of personal interest. Participating in a fun activity and helping others offer tremendous benefits in helping your mind and body to refuel.

6| Many highly-successful business people have turned to meditation to enhance overall well-being, and to recalibrate to achieve more and become more productive. Meditate for as little as five minutes and feel the positive results. Schedule it right into your calendar.

Everyone has a choice of how to use their time. It is a matter of making time to recharge a priority. You are worth it.

|| 5 Ways to Be More Interesting ||

There are numerous ways to be thought of as interesting, but most of us need to invest both time and effort to do so. What one person considers an interesting person, another might find to be a bit of a bore. Thankfully, we live in a world where there are a variety of people with various careers, hobbies, and life experiences. Explore how to become a more dynamic and interesting person.

Do you think of yourself as interesting? I hope so, but you might be in the minority. Did you base your opinion on the knowledge you have amassed, where you grew up, what you have done with your life, where you have traveled, what hobbies you have, how you have donated your time, or perhaps who you know? How often have you said to yourself, or others, "I just met the most interesting person!" If this is a frequent experience, consider yourself fortunate.

If you're like the majority of people who simply go about their daily routine, and you do not work in an industry with tons of opportunities to meet interesting people, chances are you are not putting yourself in enough situations to warrant meeting cool people. In general, if you ask someone enough questions, you are bound to learn something intriguing. Or, perhaps you are, in fact, an interesting person and either do not realize this, or give yourself credit for falling into this esteemed category.

Some people take a more calculated approach to enriching their lives, hence putting themselves into a category of being a more interesting human being. Depending upon your interests, goals, or finances, you may restrict your potential for having out-of-the-ordinary experiences. For example, when's the last time you dove in the tropics, climbed a mountain, sailed around the world, learned a new language, or had a real adventure?

Having limited funds should not be an excuse. There are a myriad of activities that cost little or no money, and can head you towards becoming a more well-rounded, fascinating person.

Here are five suggestions to help you become a more dynamic and interesting human being.

1| Think about who you find interesting. What makes them so? Could you be like them at some point in the future?

2| Lots of people talk about creating a bucket list of activities they want to do or places they wish to visit before they leave this earth. Put one together so you can have something to strive for and to talk about once you have ticked off the various items.

3| If the things you want to do cost money, start saving — set aside a separate account or lock box. Saving for things you want to do is a great way to make them happen, and ultimately an investment towards making you more interesting.

4| Are there things on your "life list" that you are afraid of doing? If you cannot get past the point of giving them a try, consider talking to a professional to work through any issues. Chances are, you might regret not doing what you always wanted to because you were afraid. Have you heard that F.E.A.R. is an acronym for *False Emotions Appearing Real*. Don't let your mind prevent the rest of your body from doing what it wants to accomplish.

5| Find a friend, family member, or work colleague who might be interested in doing the things you want to do, but like you, doesn't want to fly solo, so to speak. If you ask enough people if they want to do X, chances are you will find someone likeminded. If you are a salesperson, you already know this and should apply your sales skills to developing your interests.

There is no excuse about why you cannot invest, improve upon, or strive towards being more interesting than you are today. Everyone has an equal opportunity to invest in themselves. So, go for it: Start applying these tips and before you know it, you will be on your way towards creating the person you always knew you could be.

| 5 Tips to Prepare for Good Things to Happen |

What if every positive thing you thought about actually happened? Could you handle it? Have you thought about the possibilities of this actually happening, or perhaps even a percentage of the good things you are thinking about occurring? Get ready to start thinking positively, as you will need to be ready for when the good "what ifs" happen.

We all daydream about "what ifs;" but what if even a small percentage of the good things you imagine occurring to you either professionally or in life happened to you? Are you ready to embrace and enjoy them? Why is it that it seems some people have more good things happen to them? Are they luckier than others, or perhaps are they simply on a more positive "wavelength" that invites more fortunate circumstances?

Certainly, some people are better at planning some of their circumstances than others; but in life, some of what happens to us is outside of our control. However, I am a firm believer in how thinking positively can have a significant impact on your life. I have seen too many instances in my own life to not believe in the power of how thinking and being positive has incredible influence over your circumstances, and the reverse when I let negativity rule my thoughts.

As I have written about before, envisioning outcomes turning out positively can have an amazing influence on what happens. For example, consider how your day progresses when you leave your house in the morning in a bad mood. Doesn't it seem like more negative things happen (e.g., more traffic, your favorite parking spot is taken, they run out of your favorite muffin at the coffee shop, you show up later than you expected to)? Conversely, if you carry a great attitude with you throughout the day, doesn't it seem like everything seems to go much better for you? Stop to think about this concept, and use these tips to help you prepare for a positive outcome today.

1| Check your attitude like you would your pulse in the morning and throughout the day when you find yourself not thinking as optimistically as you could be.

2| If you are thinking negatively, stop your mind from spiraling deeper. Now, tell yourself the outcome is going to be fine and work out well. You will be pleasantly surprised at how this simple shift in your mindset can bring about a much more desirable outcome.

3| Literally stop what you are doing; if possible, step away for even as little as 2-3 minutes. Take a big breath, and then breathe in and out 10 times to the count of 10 with each breath. I'm not sure physiologically how this has such a powerful outcome, but it has worked wonders for me more times than you can imagine. Try it!

4| Write down scenarios about your "what if's" and think about how you want the circumstances to play out. When these "what ifs" happen, you will be prepared to deal with them much better, especially when they are positive "what if" scenarios.

5| Talk to someone you trust about your "what if" thinking. They might have some phenomenal suggestions you might not have considered that will enhance the outcomes of your "what ifs."

Being prepared to handle both positive and negative scenarios can serve you well. I hope the negative ones you will be thinking about don't outnumber the positive ones. If they do, I want you to start thinking about making sure your positive "what ifs" are at least a 3 to 1 ratio. Having more positive "what ifs" will make you feel much better, and have you focused on having a more pleasant professional and personal life.

‖ 6 Ways to Leverage Your Energy ‖

If you ask someone whether they are a morning or evening person, most will easily be able to tell which they tend to favor. Not everyone has ideal working hours — ones that are in alignment with their body clocks. So learn effective strategies to maximize your time.

Most of us have an internal timepiece that beats to its own circadian rhythm. And sometimes that body clock is at odds with our required work schedule.

An example of this is my brother-in-law, who is a Federal Express pilot. All of his flights take place at night. If you were to ask him whether the timing of when he has to fly is ideal, you can probably guess his answer. But his job requires him to adjust to being both a day and a night person. Since he was in the military for more than 20 years, he has more training than most people in how to make the most of less-than-desirable hours to be awake.

There are many jobs that require people to work non-traditional business hours, and for some people, it's a great choice. Some may be night owls who like being awake during the hours the majority of people are asleep. There are benefits to working non-traditional office hours, but if you are not a night person, you might find it difficult to adjust to being at the top of your game during these hours. And what if you are a night owl and at a job that requires you to work more traditional business hours, such as 8 a.m. to 5:30 p.m.? Fortunately, for those who are not morning people, there are plenty of others with whom to commiserate about being up early.

How can we cope with the times of the day when we are not feeling our most alert? Here are six ways to make the most of being a morning person, or manage mornings if you are a night owl:

1| If you are a morning person, start your day earlier than others when you are the most alert and your brain is highly engaged. I normally start my business day around 7 a.m. — earlier when I am able. This gives me as much as two to four hours to work on projects that require me to be at peak performance.

2| Schedule your day and tasks based upon completing the most challenging projects during your personal peak performance time, and the easiest projects when you are tired or not as focused.

3| Whenever possible, distribute assignments to others based on their ideal working hours. Get creative with your scheduling to make this work.

4| If your company offers flexible hours, take full advantage.

5| Don't fight your tendency to try to adjust to everyone else's peak performance schedule. Accept the fact you might not be in the same circadian rhythm as your colleagues. Come to terms with the fact you also have peak hours, which are possibly out of alignment with your team members.

6| I'm a big fan of work sprints. I remain hyper-focused on the work I am doing for short periods of time, and then take a breather. As I am on my break, I typically look forward to coming back to resuming the task. I normally reserve this type of technique when I am doing work I might not enjoy as much as other projects I also need to accomplish.

No one ever said that having perfectly sustained energy throughout the day was realistic. However, there are ways to sync your work to your body clock. See if any of these suggestions might make it feel as if you have more energy, or are more efficiently getting your work accomplished.

‖ 6 Ways to Boost Aspirational Thinking ‖

There are plenty of people to aspire to be like, but what if you are like me — someone who has always seemed to have a foggy image of who I wanted to be like? It can be important to aspire to be like someone if it helps to motivate you in some way. Who inspires you?

It's a matter of course that I aspired to be like my mother, as she is someone I have always admired for her many incredible qualities. However, a nurse, Mom was in an entirely different profession than I was, so aspiring to be like her professionally was not possible. My father was a business person, but as I have mentioned before, I still am not sure exactly what he did as he never talked about his work, so it was difficult to aspire to be just like him. So, I've aspired to have his and my mother's impressive work ethics and behavior.

As a business woman, I had very few other business women whom I could model my career on. One I can point to for inspiration, however, is Myra Hart, my first boss when I was working at the corporate headquarters of Staples. This was at the time when Staples had only four stores and was in the process of taking the office supply industry through an enormous paradigm shift.

Myra was the only c-suite female executive on the team. I carefully watched her style of interacting with other executives, and how she led our Growth and Development team. When I became a leader, I modeled my management style on what I learned from watching her.

Although other business women may have influenced me as I progressed in my management career, none became my aspirational model. This was an epiphany for me, and made me realize I had to strike out on my own and simply aspire to be the best I could be at whatever it was I was choosing to pursue , including serving as an inspirational and motivational leader for others.

Having goals and seeking inspiration can serve as your compass when you need them. You may not be in a place right now where you have a person or something to inspire you, but seek to find an aspirational model or goal.

Here are some ways to get you started:

1| Collect images that inspire you — things you aspire to possess or people you want to be like. Glue them to a paper or poster in a location you can look at often, especially on days when you need visual inspiration.

2| Create a list of people you admire, and why.

3| Create a list of activities that you aspire to accomplish.

4| Think about some of the qualities or characteristics you already possess that will help drive you towards who you aspire to be or what you strive to be doing. Chances are, you have more of them than you might think you do.

5| Have you considered whether you might be an aspirational model for someone else? Perhaps people have told you they admire you, your work or something you have a talent for. Capitalize upon these characteristics.

6| Set a realistic goal to work towards achieving what you aspire to do, and keep yourself accountable for doing so. This takes discipline, but it will be worth the commitment.

Now that you have some ideas about how to map out how to identify someone or something to aspire to, don't just give this "lip service" or put the idea on a shelf — go out and start making it happen. As the saying goes, "There is no time like the present, and the present is now."

|| 10 Advantages to Being A Mature Worker ||

If you are under 40, the thought of being considered "mature" might seem far in the future. There are many positives to getting older, but often we only hear about the negatives. But there are many benefits to aging.

By the time you reach your 30s, you have generally settled into an industry and a career. You have also, by this time, hopefully have had an opportunity to work with people who are a variety of ages. What most people do not realize, however, is how valuable mature employees with years of experience are, or how to fully tap into their potential. Our society has done a decent job of onboarding new and younger employees. Where society has failed is knowing how best to leverage the talent of the workforce over 50. Or 60. Or 70.

Recently I witnessed an incredible team effort by a group of women making gifts to be sold at a community fair. The average age of the women working together was about 70. When I walked into the holiday event a month later, where all of the incredible handmade items were on display, I felt as if I had been transported to a different and magical world. The sheer beauty of the handmade items was stunning. They were a testament to a team working together who had donated their skills and time.

Could a group of people who were younger have accomplished the same thing this group of women in their 70s, 80s, and 90s did? Sure! Age should not be a limitation in either the workplace or in life if someone is determined to participate. But due to ageism, many of our mature workers are forced out of the work place. This is such a shame. Here are ten reasons for why older workers rock:

1| Understanding what has been done in the past can be helpful in establishing current priorities. Mature employees have experience with knowing what has — and has not — worked. Knowing what to *not* focus on is an enormously valuable skill.

2| Time is our most precious asset. Most mature workers have become exceptionally good at managing their time, and know how to maximize accomplishing goals with a disciplined approach.

3| Mature workers, in general, tend to be dependable, and have built up a strong work ethic, mindset, and behavior that is valuable modeling for younger generations.

4| Having already experienced failures in their life, mature works can be much less afraid of making mistakes and taking risks, contrary to other thinking.

5| Communication skills generally improve over time, and because of this, mature workers do a better job of being able to articulate information, solve challenges, and interact with customers who can sometimes be difficult to deal with.

6| Focusing on tasks or on developing a long-range strategy becomes much easier to accomplish as you mature. You tend to take a value-driven, longer-term perspective with work strategy.

7| Knowing how to handle more interactions with both people and situations is something gained from being exposed to a variety of scenarios during one's career.

8| Having the ability to be retrospective on most matters can be quite beneficial in terms of getting beyond challenging matters sooner rather than later.

9| Patience is generally a skill developed over time. Having mature team members with an ability to not over react can help a company to remain on course and make small adjustments, versus reactive decisions that typically do not serve companies well in the long term.

10| Although there is a perception people only have high energy when they are young, mature employees might in fact have more energy. Less of their focus is on concerns such as social pressure, college loans, and raising young children, for example.

|| 10 Ways to Own Your Confidence ||

What does the term "to own" mean to you? The first thing that comes to mind is having legal possession. Another interpretation is to be highly confident in whatever it is you are pursuing, doing, or have just finished. Are you making career and life choices you are proud to own?

Possessing confidence can be one of the most satisfying feelings, especially when it's derived from something you are proud of, or enjoy doing. Demonstrating confidence to others comes in a variety of ways you present yourself — how you speak, walk, shake hands, and treat others.

Confident people have a certain allure about them that you know they have, but that is difficult to describe. You just know they have it. The funny thing about confidence is that it is a fluid feeling. When you are able to sustain confidence, it becomes more difficult to lose.

Too often I have seen people with that self-assured presence allow others to chip away at it. This generally happens when the person is in the process of building their own confidence.

Confidence is similar to creating a foundation. With proper building blocks, confidence can become a solid foundation. When we build our foundation of confidence, sometimes we choose strong substances like boulders, and sometimes we don't. This often happens as we test our ability to own something, and when we are in the process of experimenting with our confidence-building strategies. But without a load-bearing structure, it easily erodes.

How do you know whether you have built a strong confidence foundation, or one made of a weak substance, such as dust? Consider these strategies to build your confidence foundation:

1| Write down three things you are proud of having accomplished. These do not have to be monumental achievements, and can be divided into both professional and personal accomplishments.

2| On a scale of 1-5, how would your rate your accomplishments?

3| Think about how you can continue to build upon the accomplishments you have achieved. Putting it in writing makes it more likely to happen.

4| Now, jot down three or more things you want to accomplish professionally or personally in the next year, or sooner.

5| In just a few sentences, plot out how you are going to be able to accomplish the things you want to do. This does not have to be an exercise in crafting a novel, and only you need to see this information.

6| Ask a half dozen of your colleagues to to email you three or more words that describe who you are. Offer to reciprocate. In fact, you may want to do that first!

7| Once you have a list of words, use this information to gain insight into how others view you. Part of this exercise is to demonstrate that other people may see you in a much stronger position professionally than you see yourself.

8| Commit to doing at least one random act of kindness every day. These small gestures will indirectly help to build your confidence as you will feel more satisfied by doing something nice for others. The feeling will be cumulative and help to strengthen the confidence foundation you are building.

9| Make sure every day you have an opportunity to work on doing the things that make you feel confident. Just like a physical workout, each time you do this is equivalent to building the core strength of your confidence muscle, which you absolutely want to fully OWN.

10| We've all heard the expression, "Fake it 'til you make it." There is something interesting about this expression. Part of it has to do with acting confident, even when you may not feel that way. Whether it's giving a presentation, going after your dream job, planning an event, or doing research, if you have not already tried applying this concept, please do! Before you know it, you will not feel like you are faking it anymore.

‖ 10 Tips on Living Without Regrets ‖

Is it possible to live a life with no regrets? It might be, but one thing seems to consistently get in the way — our minds. If you could turn off your mind from processing and delivering thoughts related to being regretful, that would make your career or life more satisfying.

No one is immune from having a few regrets. The good news is that you have the power to change your decision-making process to ensure fewer future regrets either personally or professionally.

Some of the regrets people have are due to making mistakes. Sometimes the mistakes made were due to inexperience, immaturity, being in the wrong place at the wrong time, or a myriad of other reasons. The point is, you first need to stop ruminating on the mistakes. You must not continue to harbor regretful thinking about them. Sure, some of the regrets you have could be monumental ones, but sometimes we are regretful about minor decisions and outcomes from our actions.

The feeling of being regretful can weigh us down unnecessarily, and can be "baggage" that keeps us from being more nimble with future decision making, and more conservative and restrictive than we might need to be. Sound familiar?

The fact you have regrets makes you human. At some point, it's essential to come to terms with your regrets, even if they have impacted others. It is also not mentally healthy to constantly challenge yourself and question all of your future decisions based on a collection of regrets. Here are 10 ways to help shed your regrets and move on with life:

1| Make a list of what you want to accomplish. Include both short- and long-term goals. Separate this list into two parts — one for your personal life, the other for your professional one.

2| Write down a list of the instances about which you are regretful. Then, write why you regret what you did.

3| Leveraging your regret list, design a scenario of what you would have done differently if you could wind back time and hit the re-do button.

4| Do any of the regrets you have involve needing to apologize to someone or a group of people? If so, make plans to apologize to the people you impacted, and do it within the next month.

5| Give yourself a couple of days to mourn your regrets, and then move on. The things you are regretful about are not going to change, but you can change the way you think about your regrets.

6| Pick a day in the next month when you are going to commit to stop allowing your mind to focus on your regrets. Once this day comes, tell yourself you no longer need to keep applying your mental resources and energy towards your regretful thinking.

7| Talk to someone you trust about your regrets, and have them provide you with insight into — on a scale of 1-5 — what level they would apply to the topics you are regretful about. You might be surprised how much weight you have assigned to a regret that in other people's opinions are much less impactful than you think they are.

8| Make a deal with yourself to change your perspective and to stick with your new, more positive outlook, based on how your trusted advisor rated them.

9| Commit to helping someone else professionally or personally to overcome the regrets they are carrying around.

10| If you cannot mentally get past the regrets you have, and you have never spoken to someone professionally about this, perhaps it's time to seek counseling to help work through your stumbling blocks.

Show me someone who claims to have a perfect, regret-free life and I will flat out tell you they are lying — if not to you, then to themselves. Everyone has regrets in their life. How you come to terms with them will set you up to have a much healthier and interesting life centered around creating the life you always dreamed you could have.

‖ 5 Ways to Maximize Your Time ‖

Time is precious; yet some of us take it for granted. Being blasé is not something we mean to do, but it happens. If you knew how much time you had left, would you look at life and what you do differently?

Everyone has the same amount of time to work with each day — 24 hours, but some use it better than others. Have some people figured out how to better optimize their work hours with advanced time management skills? How is it they are more cognizant of how precious time is? Others may not give the concept more than a fleeting thought and consequently, do not use their time constructively. Here are my top inhibitors to provide insight into why some of us fail at being productive:

- A skewed perception of time because of a limiting belief that there is an unlimited supply;

- A lack of awareness of schedules or deadlines that offers a false sense of having more time than they actually do;

- No command of time management practices, either because they haven't developed any, or because they have not considered this an essential life skill to master;

- A lack of motivation that prevents highlighting the importance of maximizing time; and

- An inability to discern the passing of time.

Our minds work better and we tend to have increased energy when we have a command of our time. Use these five simple ways to reconsider how you spend your time and learn to be more productive:

1| Create a weekly schedule. It does not have to be detailed. But do factor in activities such as exercise, preparation of healthy meals, and mini mental health breaks.

2| At the end of each month, create a list of goals you want to accomplish either professionally or personally the next month. The list does not have to be outrageous. Include both attainable short- and long-term goals.

3| Think about how you are currently using your time. Are you simply going through the motions of waking up, going to work, coming home, and hitting *repeat*? If this is the case, think about incorporating some activities into your day that you can eagerly anticipate. Having something to look forward to is highly motivating.

4| Break your day into segments. I'm a morning person, so when I know I have to get something done that is not a task I enjoy, or one that requires intense concentration, I plan to get it finished ASAP. Granted, you do not always have control over the ideal time to get things done; but if you can divide each day into planned segments you will find you will get more accomplished.

5| Build rewards into your schedule. Make sure your day is broken up with activities such as taking a walk, getting a cup of coffee, or spending a limited time on social media to catch up on current events. Include time to interact socially with co-workers or friends — or perhaps a mix of the two ... who knows what will happen!

‖ 5 Tips to Stepping Out of Your Comfort Zone ‖

Most people are not that eager to push themselves too far. Sure, you might think you are a tough dude or chick; but I guarantee you can do even more than you think. The challenges need not be created or accomplished daily. The point is to get out of your comfort zone! It's easier than it looks.

Too many people settle into life and then get stuck. Then they wonder why others are surpassing them professionally. Hint: not enough personal challenges.

Someone once said that success begins at the end of your comfort zone. Do you believe that's true? Once most people finish something, they generally will take a break from whatever it was they accomplished. This is perfectly understandable and acceptable. But successful people are always learning new things and challenging themselves.

You do not have to be competitive by nature to want to expand your mind and abilities. Learning should not be parked at the door once we graduate from a program, but many people accept their accomplishment as permission to hit the snooze button on life.

Why do people fall into the trap of becoming too comfortable? Part of it has to do with the fact that they may not be naturally enamored by success. Truthfully, I cannot imagine working without having goals, and I am constantly amazed when I learn about people who do not have strategic markers to achieve. Actually, I am not sure how anything gets done, or that the right items are focused on without having targets in place for everyone.

So, what if you are working at a company that does not set goals? Start by asking your boss to schedule a meeting to develop your goals. Ask how performance is measured. There are some positions where it may not make sense to have traditional goals. Instead, set goals based upon measurements, such as customer satisfaction, work performance, and overall project results. Marketing and sales teams typically have quarterly goals, so people in these roles are accustomed to having to reach milestones, but this does not mean they are still challenging themselves beyond the performance benchmarks being set for them.

The goals being set for you do not have to be the only ones you have to achieve. You should have your own set of personal goals (e.g., saving for a vacation, hitting a personal best record at your favorite sport, volunteering a certain number of hours per month). The point is, you have more time than you think to fit in things that are part of helping you to reach your goals. You simply need to reprioritize how you allocate your time.

When you consider how you can really challenge yourself, ponder these five points. Your responses will help move you out of your comfort zone, and on your way to accomplishing more than you imagined was possible.

1| Stop procrastinating. Limit social media interactions, gaming, or whatever it is that consumes hours of your time and results in nothing tangible.

2| Make a list of what you want to accomplish in the next year, then break those goals into the months you plan to complete them.

3| Work backwards from the goals you set and list the steps needed to reach them.

4| Are the goals you set realistic? Don't create too many and set yourself up for failure, but do look to push yourself beyond what you think you can achieve. Make sure you keep tabs on how you are doing each month and how close you are to reaching your milestones and eventually your destination.

5| Establish a reward system for reaching each step along the path. Most humans are intrinsically driven by rewards, so make sure you build some treats into your system. Once you achieve your goals, set new ones, and look forward to achieving them. After going through this process for three to six months, the process of working on and achieving goals will come naturally.

These are just a few ideas that can help you to break out of your comfort zone and begin accomplishing more than you ever imagined.

| 5 Ways to Find Your Confidence |

Some people seem to be born with confidence. For those who were not, confidence can be developed over time, through various methods. If you are not one of the people graced with the confidence gene at birth, take heart. There are techniques you can use to increase your confidence quotient.

How is it that some people seem to exude confidence, while others are on a perpetual journey to find it? If you are one of the people not as confident as you would like to be, or feel like you are faking your confidence most of the time, you are not alone. However, there are things you can do to boost and maintain your confidence.

If you've been following my writing for any length of time, you can probably guess whether I was blessed with the confidence gene. (I was!) As I meet and talk to new people, I am often stunned when the ones who come across as being particularly self-assured often share with me that they wish they were more confident. This is an indication that it is easier to fake your confidence until it feels real. I'm not advocating being inauthentic, but you have certainly heard the expression, "Fake it until you make it."

Having confidence allows you to pursue things others might not. People who possess confidence come across differently than people who have not yet found and harnessed theirs. Of course, it is possible to be confident about some things and not others. The trick is to work towards being more confident in a number of categories and not just a few.

Becoming completely confident can take time. There is no particular formula to calculate how quickly you can gain your confidence.

The good news is that one day you will simply realize you are either almost fully confident, or exponentially more self-assured than you were. Here's how:

1| Focus on something you like to do. Now think about how it makes you feel. Have people told you that you are good at "fill-in-the-blank?" Hearing you are proficient at something can help to build your confidence.

2| Develop skills in areas you are currently working on, especially if they are skills you enjoy doing. If you do not enjoy applying the skills you use in your life or career, I encourage you to rethink why you are doing what you are doing. Of course, there are aspects of every job or life skills we may not enjoy; but some of the ones we enjoy doing the least could potentially be done by someone else at some point. When you further develop skills you are currently working on, and gain mastery of them, you will bolster your confidence.

3| Help others with the skills you have mastered. Doing this will make you feel proud, and in turn, more confident.

4| Ask others who know you well what they think is something you do that showcases your confidence. You might already be exhibiting signs of confidence.

5| Think about the people you admire and what makes them appear confident. Until you get there yourself, you can imitate what they are doing until you have more faith in your own abilities.

There are benefits to being confident: One is you come across as likeable; another, which everyone likes, is that you are more interesting, and potentially more desirable.

Your confidence will inspire others to follow and get to know more about you. Don't be surprised if people go out of their way to become your friend. Confident people tend to have more friends, more opportunities, and can enjoy an enriched life.

Let's increase your confidence, as the benefits of having more faith and trust in your own abilities are worth the effort! Oh, and if you need an extra boost of confidence, just listen to the song "I Have Confidence" from *The Sound of Music*. [Adjust lyrics to fit your personal situation.]

|| Bibliography ||

Byrne, Rhonda. *The Secret.* New York (NY): Atria Publishing Group, 2006.

Fulghum, Robert. *All I Really Need To Know I Learned in Kindergarten.* New York (NY): Villard Books, 1988.

Rath, Tom. *Strengths Finder 2.0.* Washington, DC: Gallup Press, 2007.

Rodgers, Richard, and Hammerstein II, Oscar. "I Have Confidence." *The Sound of Music.* November 16, 1959: Lunt-Fontanne Theatre, New York, NY

|| Index ||

‖ Market Me Too — List of Services ‖

- Coaching
- Workshops
- Speaking
- Team Strengths Reveal (TSR)
- On-line Courses
- Consulting

Benefits From Working With Us

We provide our clients with new insight into how to think, act, and perform in their roles or on their teams. Equipped with a new understanding of their unique strengths and how to best apply them, our clients are then able to implement these insights to boost individual or team performance goals. This is a winning combination for everyone.

Coaching Services

> **Individual Coaching** focuses on recognizing, embracing, and applying strategies to maximize your strengths and talents.

> **Executive Coaching** provides new insights into how to further leverage your management talents professionally, and for the benefit of those you lead.

> **Family Coaching** improves your family unity and dynamics.

> **Work and Sports Team Coaching** utilizes team performance coaching to help each member gain insight into how they contribute to the team, and how by working together differently, they can accelerate performance results and be more satisfied in their respective roles. By focusing leaders and teams on how to better leverage the raw and natural talents on their team, they are optimally enabled to reach specific individual and team performance goals. Team coaching options include **Team Rebuild, Energize & Optimize, New, and Pairing.**

Other Services

Workshops – Our workshops are highly interactive, fun, and impactful, and include topics such as **Communication, Culture, Leadership, Motivation,** and **Productivity.** Contact me for a complete list of workshops, or to discuss creating a custom workshop for your company.

Online Course(s) – Our courses are available via the Mighty Networks Learning Platform under the name "Wisdom Whisperer," and listed on MarketMeToo.net.

Keynote & Professional Speaker – Please contact me about your speaking requirements.

TV Show & Podcast – "Murf & E Unfiltered – Zero BS Biz Talk." TV (Via YouTube)

Interested? Let's Talk!

To learn more or discuss your consulting needs, call (339) 987-0195, email KathyMurphy@me.com, or visit my website at MarketMeToo.net.

Coming in 2021!

Next in the WISDOM WHISPERER Series

For More Information, visit MarketMeToo.net